P9-CFG-272

THE
PRESSURED
COOK

THE PRESSURED COOK

OVER 75 ONE-POT MEALS IN MINUTES

MADE IN TODAY'S 100% SAFE PRESSURE COOKERS

LORNA SASS

WILLIAM MORROW AND COMPANY, INC. / NEW YORK

Library of Congress Cataloging-in-Publication Data

Sass, Lorna J.
    The pressured cook : over 75 one-pot meals in minutes made in today's 100% safe pressure cookers / Lorna Sass. — 1st ed.
        p.   cm.
    Includes index.
    ISBN 0-688-15828-5
    1. Pressure cookery.   I. Title.
TX840.P7S36324   1998
641.5'87—dc21   98-38885
                                                       CIP

Printed in the United States of America   *641.587*
                                            SAS

FIRST EDITION

1   2   3   4   5   6   7   8   9   10

BOOK DESIGN BY GRETCHEN ACHILLES

www.williammorrow.com

TO MY ELVES

WITH HEARTFELT THANKS

AND

TO ALL THOSE WHO STILL BELIEVE IN HOME COOKING

CONTENTS

ACKNOWLEDGMENTS

Although my name is on the cover of this book, the efforts of many kind and enthusiastic people enrich these pages.

Writing and recipe development are solitary tasks, but cooking becomes joyously communal when I am regularly in contact with my family of elves—my term of endearment for the old and newfound friends all over the country who have tested these recipes many times over. They often sent me back to the kitchen or computer in search of better flavor, more accessible ingredients, and simplified instructions. Thanks to them, you can count on these recipes not only to taste good, but to work in any brand of cooker.

My gratitude and blessings to the following elves: Judy Bloom, Heather and Gerhard Bock, Munro Bonnell, Joan Carlton, Dena Cherenson, Arlene Ciroula, Joyce Curwin, Christian Dorbandt, Martine Gérard, Dennis Hunsicker, Barbara Kirshenblatt-Gimblett, Michele Lunt, Elizabeth Moffett, Joanne Moore, Greg Mowery, Banoo Parpia, Mary Ellen Power, Ken and Catherine Ryan, Marty Sass, Rachael Shapiro, Sandra Shapiro, Phyllis Simons, and Allyne Smith.

For their efforts above and beyond, heartfelt thanks to SUPER elves Cathy Roberts for giving detailed feedback on every recipe, for making dozens of cheesecakes and bread puddings, and most importantly for becoming such a gentle, knowing midwife to the entire book; Rosemary Serviss for her meticulous attention to the vegetarian one-pots; and Alisa Zlotnikoff for her cheerful kitchen companionship and dessert expertise.

Colleagues Elizabeth Germain, Elizabeth Schneider, Barbara Spiegel, Michele Urvater, and Cathy Walthers shared their culinary expertise with enthusiasm and open-hearted generosity. Justin Schwartz, my editor at William Morrow, has been the most efficient and responsive E-mail buddy an author could ever wish for. Culinary tours of Crete, Tunisia, and Liguria hosted by Oldways Preservation Exchange & Trust offered delicious inspiration.

Fun adviser and special sweetie, Richard Isaacson, provided irresistible and very necessary breaks from life under pressure.

A HEALTHY NEW DEFINITION
OF FAST FOOD

"There is a gadget on the market that permits a cook to scoff at time. It is a pressure cooker . . . The hurry-up cook in possession of this steamer may serve many dishes denied her by any other method."

—IRMA S. ROMBAUER
Joy of Cooking (1946 edition)

Turkey chili in three minutes? Risotto in five and Moroccan chicken in twelve? How about fork-tender brisket in under an hour?

The pressure cooker has changed my life, and it will change yours too. This marvelous appliance cooks in one-third or less the standard cooking time and serves forth delicious versions of all those long-simmered foods you've been hankering after. Few cooks nowadays have the requisite three hours to make a pot roast or corned beef. But with an hour and a pressure cooker, these all-American favorites can once again become regulars on your menu.

It's been over a decade since I bought my first pressure cooker and was introduced to a healthy new definition of fast food. I quickly became intrigued and spent a year developing recipes for the book that became *Cooking Under Pressure*. When that book came out in 1989, many people were afraid of pressure cookers.

But over the last decade I've watched that fear steadily fade away. Word has gotten out that the new generation of cookers is completely safe and easy to use. Futhermore, what was once a casual interest in speed cooking has become a pressing need.

In this book I've taken pressure cooking a step farther by creating whole meals in one pot, saving you not only oodles of cooking time, but lots of cleanup as well. As you cook your way through these recipes, you'll get vibrant tastes of faraway places, from the Mediterranean to Asia, from India to Ethiopia and Latin America. You'll also find down-home American dishes like chili, gumbo, and succotash.

And, for those who don't consider a meal complete without a sweet, I've included some sensational desserts. So why not try these tasty, home-cooked dishes and join the growing number of pressured cooks who have learned the secret of scoffing at time? Happy cooking!

—LORNA SASS
New York City

If you need information on purchasing a pressure cooker or would like to share your recipes or reactions for the next edition of this book, I'd be happy to hear from you. (Please enclose a SASE if requesting a response.) Write to me c/o Cooking Under Pressure, POB 704, New York, NY 10024.

PRESSURE COOKING PERFECTED

This chapter explains the basics. If you're experienced with pressure cooking, feel free to skip ahead to the sections called "What Else Do I Need?" and "Before You Begin, Read This." Then head for the kitchen.

If you've never cooked under pressure before, take a few moments to read this chapter and the introductory booklet that came with your pressure cooker. If you are one of those folks who experience new appliance phobia, please rest assured that after cooking under pressure once or twice, you'll feel quite at ease with this remarkable kitchen tool. Indeed, you'll wonder how you ever managed without it.

GETTING STARTED

Check the manufacturer's instruction booklet and take note of the following:

1. How high you can fill your cooker with ingredients. (This amount is referred to as the "maximum capacity.")

2. How to lock the lid in place.

3. How to know when the cooker has reached high pressure.

4. How to quick-release the pressure right on the stovetop, without setting the cooker under cold running water. (Some cookers do not have this option.)

5. How to unlock the lid once all of the pressure has been released.

How Does the Pressure Cooker Work?

Once the lid is locked into place and the cooker is set over high heat, the liquid inside comes to a boil and produces steam. This steam is trapped inside the sealed pot, forcing the pressure to build to 15 pounds above normal sea-level pressure. Under 15 pounds of pressure, water boils at 250°F rather than the standard 212°F. At this higher-than-normal boiling point, the fiber in food breaks down and the flavors mingle in one-third or less the standard cooking time.

For the pressure cooker to work properly, there must be sufficient room inside the pot for the steam pressure to build. Therefore, cookers may be filled anywhere from halfway to three-quarters of total capacity, depending upon the type of ingredients and the particular design.

Once high pressure is reached, you must lower the heat to prevent excess buildup of pressure. If you forget to lower the heat, the pressure cooker will remind you by making loud, hissing sounds.

A New Generation of Safe Cookers

While you are probably aware of American-made Presto and Mirro pressure cookers, you may not know that many housewares departments now stock a new and improved style of cooker imported from Europe. These sleek and sophisticated appliances—what I refer to as second-generation pressure cookers—have stationary pressure regulators rather than removable jiggle-tops.

While most pressure cookers now on the market (both first and second generation) are completely safe and have been redesigned with one or more backup mechanisms to prevent excess buildup of pressure, here are some advantages to the second-generation cookers:

User-Friendly: There's no guessing about when you've reached high pressure since it's indicated by a line on the pressure rod.

Better Construction: Most cookers are made of high-quality stainless steel (rather than aluminum) and have a layer of copper or aluminum in the bottom for even cooking—especially important for prevention of scorching when bringing up the pressure over high heat. Also, the design of the pressure rod eliminates concerns about clogging the vent, making it possible to cook foaming foods like beans and grains without careful monitoring.

Peace and Quiet: These cookers don't make any chug-chug sounds and hiss only to warn you that the heat's too high.

If your local housewares store doesn't have a range of cookers to choose from, you might want to inquire directly from the manufacturers to compare designs and prices. For a directory of toll-free telephone numbers, see page 247.

What Size Cooker Is Best?

The recipes in this collection have all been tested in a 6-quart cooker, the size I recommend for the average cook. If you wish to cook in quantity or regularly make broths, opt for an 8-quart. (Imported European cookers are sized in liters. A 5-liter cooker holds approximately 6 quarts; a 7-liter cooker holds approximately 8 quarts.)

The pot sizes I'm suggesting may strike you as rather large, but keep in mind that the cooker cannot be filled more than three-quarters full (or halfway when cooking beans and grains) to allow sufficient room for the steam pressure to build.

Can I Use My Old Jiggle-Top Cooker?

If this book has inspired you to retrieve your old jiggle-top cooker from the basement or you purchase one of the more affordable jiggle-top models, you can successfully cook the recipes in this book.

If your cooker hasn't been used in a while, it may need a new gasket (the rubber ring that fits inside the lid and seals the cooker). Test the gasket by placing 2 cups of water in the cooker and bringing it up to pressure. If water drips down the sides of the pot or the pressure doesn't rise, purchase a new gasket. Do not attempt to use any gasket except the one made for your model. If you can't find a replacement gasket at your local housewares store, check directly with the manufacturer (see page 247 for telephone numbers).

When cooking foods that create excessive foam—such as beans and grains—always add at least 2 teaspoons of oil to keep the foam under control. Since preparing these foods is usually cautioned against by manufacturers, be sure to remain in the kitchen while they are cooking. If any loud hissing occurs, turn off the heat and release the pressure by setting the cooker under cold running water. Remove the lid and check the vent for any bits of clogged food, then clean the lid thoroughly. Add another tablespoon of oil, return to high pressure, and continue cooking.

During cooking, jiggle-top cookers tend to vent more steam and therefore lose more liquid. If you consistently experience dry results, increase the liquid recommended in the recipe by quarter-cup increments until you discover the right formula for your cooker.

Some jiggle-top cookers are aluminum and have thin bottoms. If you experience scorching, get into the habit of using a Flame Tamer (see page 4).

What Else Do I Need?

Using a **timer** is the key to carefree pressure cooking. I like the three-way elec-
tronic timer made by West Bend (item number 40032) because I'm often cooking
more than one dish at a time. If you are content with your oven or watch timer,
you're all set.

A **garlic press** is indispensable when adding garlic at the end of cooking as
many recipes recommend. A good press will virtually peel and mash each
unpeeled clove with one squeeze, extruding a puree that quickly infuses the dish
with flavor. When using the press, squeeze it right over the cooker and use a paring knife to scrape the puree directly into the pot. Then use the tip of the knife
to poke the peel out of the bowl of the press and discard it. (Any mashed bits of
pulp still in the press may be added to the cooker.) Not all garlic presses are well
designed. I recommend the Swiss-made Zyliss Susi, available from Zabar's (see
Mail-Order Sources, page 245), or call 714-858-5005 to locate a local source.

A 4-cup or larger **gravy separator** is essential for degreasing stews when
you don't have time to refrigerate them overnight. The well-designed long spout
extending from the base of the separator allows you to easily pour off degreased
gravy, leaving behind a layer of fat that rises to the top.

If your cooker doesn't have a well-constructed bottom or the bottom
scorches, you'll want to purchase a **Flame Tamer**, an inexpensive round metal
disc that diffuses heat. It is available in any well-stocked kitchen store. To use
this diffuser, preheat it for one minute over high heat. Set the cooker on the
Flame Tamer and bring it up to pressure. (This will take a few minutes longer
than if the cooker were directly over the flame but will not critically affect the
cooking time.) Once the cooker is up to pressure, lower the heat to maintain high
pressure and continue cooking on the Flame Tamer. Remove the cooker from the
Flame Tamer before letting the pressure come down naturally or using a quick-
release method.

You'll need a porcelain or glass 1½- or 2-quart **soufflé dish** or **heatproof
casserole** if you wish to make bread puddings. The cheesecake recipe requires
a small **springform pan,** approximately 7 inches in diameter. If you have trouble finding these two items in your local cookware shop, they can be mail-
ordered from Zabar's (page 246). Make sure that each of these fits into the
cooker with at least a half inch to spare around the perimeter, and have heavy-
duty aluminum foil on hand for wrapping them securely before cooking.

Both the soufflé dish and springform pan must be set on a **trivet**. If your
cooker doesn't come with a trivet, you can improvise one by turning the steam-

ing basket upside down or forming aluminum foil into a log and shaping the log into a ring that fits snugly inside the cooker.

I also recommend a **minichopper/immersion blender**. Although I'm not a fan of small electrics, I'm in love with my Braun hand blender with chopper attachment (MR 360). It allows me to puree all or part of a soup right in the cooker, and does a terrific job of mincing ginger and garlic (which you will soon discover I use with abandon). It is reasonably good at grinding spices, but I opt for a coffee grinder (set aside for this purpose) when I want my spices really finely ground.

A **kitchen scale** is very handy for weighing vegetables (and outgoing mail). **Long-handled wooden spoons** are ideal for stirring ingredients in the deep cooker. A **long-handled large ladle** is great for serving most of the recipes in this book. **Long-handled tongs** are useful when roasting red peppers over gas burners.

Caring for the Cooker

Pressure cookers don't require much more maintenance than the average pot, but here are a few details to consider:

Removing and Cleaning the Gasket: Do this after each use. To preserve the life of the rubber gasket, allow it to air-dry thoroughly before setting it back in the lid. Although gaskets last for years, it's wise to have a backup on hand for the moment when the rubber gives out.

Cleaning the Vent/Valve Area: Whenever you wash the lid, take a quick look at this area and, if needed, scrub it free of debris with a soapy scouring pad or toothbrush. If you have a second-generation cooker, from time to time—especially if your cooker is not functioning properly—unscrew the pressure regulator and wash the parts well. (Look for detailed instructions in the owner's manual.) When reassembling the parts, be sure the screw is good and tight.

Cleaning the Bottom: If the bottom is scorched, sprinkle on some scouring cleanser such as Bon Ami, add about 2 cups of water, and bring to a boil in the cooker. Remove from the heat and let sit for a few hours or overnight. Scrub clean with a scouring pad.

Shining the Cooker: If you like to keep your pots looking spanking new, try a product called Bar Keepers Friend. Although this cleanser and polisher claims to be "best since 1882," I've only recently discovered how terrific it is. (To locate a source in your area, call 800-433-5818.)

Storing: Rest the lid against the side of the cooker or set it upside down on top of the pot. If the gasket isn't thoroughly dry, drape it loosely on the lid. Avoid locking the lid in place for storage or you'll be greeted by a strong whiff of your last meal when you next open the cooker.

THE LANGUAGE OF PRESSURE COOKING

Here are explanations of the phrases you will encounter time and again in the recipes. After reading them, you'll have a clear picture of what's involved in cooking under pressure.

Lock the Lid in Place: After the ingredients are assembled in the cooker, nest the lid into the pot, using arrows or other visual cues provided by the manufacturer. Turn the lid until the lid and pot handles line up. Some cookers have an additional locking mechanism—you push a small lever into place. Check your instruction booklet for specifics. Most cookers are designed so that if the lid is not properly locked in place, the pressure won't rise.

Over High Heat: High pressure is achieved as rapidly as possible by setting the cooker over maximum heat. Depending upon the quantity and type of food you are cooking and the size of the cooker, it can take from 30 seconds to 20 minutes for the cooker to reach high pressure. This process can be speeded up considerably by adding a boiling (rather than cold or room temperature) liquid. Although some cooking takes place as high pressure is approached, this period of time is not traditionally calculated as part of cooking time.

Bring to High Pressure: Check your manufacturer's instruction booklet to determine when high pressure has been reached. For second-generation cookers, high pressure is indicated by a line on the stationary pressure rod. For jiggle-top cookers, high pressure is generally indicated by a gentle rocking of the regulator. Although some cookers offer a choice of settings, all recipes in this book have been tested under high pressure (13 to 15 pounds, depending on your brand).

Lower the Heat Just Enough to Maintain High Pressure: Once high pressure is reached, lower the heat immediately; otherwise, the pressure will continue to rise, causing loud hissing sounds. After using your cooker a few times, you'll know how much heat is required to maintain high pressure. For most cookers, a flame akin to simmering is just right.

If you notice that the pressure has fallen, assume you've lowered the heat too much. If this happens, simply bring the pressure back up to high over high heat and lower the heat again. A brief period of lower pressure is not likely to affect the timing or the quality of the finished product.

Cook Under High Pressure for X Minutes: Unless otherwise noted, cooking time is calculated from the moment high pressure is reached. For example, above each recipe you'll see a phrase such as "3 minutes high pressure." This means that as soon as the cooker reaches high pressure, you set the timer and cook under high pressure for 3 minutes.

Quick-Release the Pressure: When the timer goes off, bring down the pressure by placing the cooker under cold running water. It's best to tilt the cooker about 45 degrees and run the water down one side of the cover, directing it away from the pressure vents and rod or regulator.

Second-generation cookers offer a quick-release method that can be used without moving the pot from the stove. Check the manufacturer's instruction booklet for details. Some cooks find this a practical alternative, while others don't enjoy the steam bath it sends forth.

Quick-Release the Pressure by Setting the Cooker under Cold Running Water: When I am specific about suggesting that you release pressure this way, it is because a stovetop quick-release method will cause sputtering at the vent. Sputtering generally happens when the cooker is very full or when you are cooking ingredients that foam, such as barley or split peas.

Let the Pressure Drop Naturally: When the timer goes off, turn off the heat (if using an electric stove, move the cooker to another burner) and let the cooker sit until the pressure drops of its own accord. Depending upon the quantity and type of food in the pot, this can take from 3 to 20 minutes. The food continues to cook as the pressure drops. (I generally calculate a 10-minute natural pressure release to be the equivalent of 4 minutes of cooking under pressure.) Some foods, particularly beef, require a natural pressure release to remain tender.

Some recipes call for a partial natural pressure release. For example, when a recipe says to "let the pressure come down naturally for 10 minutes," keep the lid in place for as long as indicated, whether or not the pressure has already dropped. Release any remaining pressure before attempting to remove the lid.

When overcooking is not a danger, some recipes offer you the option of quick or natural pressure release. If time permits, I recommend that you choose the natural pressure release. Although I can't prove it, I believe that the flavors and textures of food benefit from this approach. It is a gentler way to bring down the pressure—an obvious advantage when cooking beans which otherwise tend to "lose their skins."

Return to High Pressure for X Minutes: When foods are considerably underdone, it's most efficient to finish cooking under pressure. When I suggest returning to high pressure, it is understood that you must first lock the lid in place, set the cooker over high heat, and proceed as usual.

Set (But Do Not Lock) the Lid in Place and Cook for a Minute or Two in the Residual Heat: When delicate foods such as rice or fresh vegetables are only slightly underdone after the pressure is released, set the lid in place but do not align the lid and cooker handles. Let the food cook in the heat that remains in the pot until the food is done.

BEFORE YOU BEGIN, READ THIS

Generally speaking, pressure cooking resembles standard stovetop cooking, but there are some significant differences:

No Peeking: Once the lid is locked in place and the pressure is up, you can't look inside and check how things are going. It's necessary to bring the pressure down to assess doneness or add more ingredients.

Size of Ingredients: Since it's not convenient to add ingredients along the way, those with longer cooking times are cut into smaller pieces so that they will be tender when quicker-cooking ingredients are done. Alternatively, to avoid overcooking, sometimes carrots and potatoes are cooked in large chunks and then cut up after cooking. For these reasons, the ingredients list will usually specify the size or shape of an item; however, you do not need to be compulsive about the recommendations. For example, as long as the pieces of potato are roughly equal in size, they will cook properly. For a convenient built-in ruler that approximates an inch, use the area from the tip of your thumb to the first knuckle.

Flavor: The high heat in the cooker mutes the flavor of garlic, herbs, and some spices (cayenne, cumin, and cinnamon are notable exceptions). The recipes often call for whole spices because their flavors survive more successfully than ground. In addition, you'll be asked to add a larger quantity of seasoning than you may be accustomed to using. When their full flavor is required, garlic, herbs, and spices are added at the end for a final few minutes of simmering after the pressure is released.

The alcohol in wine can impart a sour taste to the dish when cooked under pressure. For this reason, when wine is used in a recipe, all of the alcohol should be burned off before the lid is locked in place.

When ingredients are submerged in liquid, their flavors quickly mingle. Foods set on top of the liquid maintain more of their individual tastes.

Color: While carrots and red peppers hold their color beautifully, greens such as kale and collards turn olive-green under pressure. If you wish to preserve their bright color, stir them in at the end and cook until tender. For visual appeal, the recipes usually call for an ingredient or garnish with vibrant color to be added just before serving.

Liquid: Most cookers require at least one cup of liquid to create the steam needed to bring up the pressure. This liquid may be in the form of water, broth, wine, or even the juices released by vegetables as they cook. Because the pressure cooker is a sealed pot, little or none of the liquid is lost during cooking. Indeed, unless you are cooking dried ingredients such as grains or unsoaked beans, you will often end up with more liquid than you added at the start. This is because many ingredients—such as onions, celery, mushrooms, and meat—release liquid as they are cooking.

About the Recipes

Cooker Size: Quantities are calculated to work in a 6-quart cooker. If you own an 8-quart model, follow the recipes as directed. Since the larger cooker will take slightly longer to come up to pressure, reduce cooking time under pressure by a minute or two when preparing delicate ingredients such as quick-cooking vegetables. If you are using a 4-quart cooker or wish to prepare a smaller quantity, simply divide the recipe in half.

Cooking Time: Cooking time under pressure is indicated at the top of each recipe for ready reference. Since personal taste and performance of cookers and ingredients differ, I have leaned in the direction of undercooking slightly. It's a simple matter either to bring the pressure back up (if the ingredients need much more cooking) or to finish them off by stovetop simmering (if they are nearly done). When ingredients are added at the end, I've indicated how much additional cooking time is required. For the sake of simplicity, I have not calculated the time it takes to brown ingredients or to bring the cooker up to pressure.

Fans of *Cooking Under Pressure* may notice slightly increased cooking times. Animals are being bred leaner nowadays; as a result it takes a bit longer to tenderize the meat.

When cooking at high altitudes, increase cooking time by 10 percent for every 2,000 feet above sea level. Microwave fans take note: Time under pressure **is not** affected by the quantity of food in the cooker.

Browning: Many recipes call for browning the meat before adding the other ingredients. There are two keys to successful browning: Never crowd the pot (there should always be space between pieces); and wait until the added oil is good and hot before browning the second or third batch.

Since the pressure cooker has high sides, it's not the ideal shape for browning. If you don't mind using a second pot, brown the meat in a large sauté pan. Use the wine or broth to scrape up any browned bits from the bottom, transfer the liquid and browned meat to the cooker, and proceed as directed.

Ingredients: Ingredients are listed in order of use. For maximum time efficiency, prepare the ingredients to be added at the end while the basic ingredients are cooking. Consult the Guide to Ingredients (page 233) for details on the selection and handling of individual items.

Scorching: Because such intense heat is used to bring the ingredients up to pressure, a few safeguards are required to avoid scorching the internal bottom of the cooker:

Many recipes call for an initial browning of meat, onions, and garlic followed by the addition of wine or broth. When the liquid is added, it is important to scrape up any bits of food sticking to the bottom of the cooker. Be careful to keep sugar- or protein-rich ingredients like pasta sauce, tomatoes, or yogurt from direct contact with the bottom by pouring them on top of other ingredients. Refrain from stirring.

Serving Sizes: This is always a tricky area since what's just enough for one person can be far too much for another. In giving estimates, I have taken into consideration that the dish in question is the main (and probably only) dish of the meal—perhaps accompanied by a salad. When in doubt, I have overestimated portion size so that you will never be caught short and may have bonus leftovers.

Preparing in Advance and Storing: Unlike many foods, most of the soups and stews in this book actually taste better when prepared ahead. In the case of many meat dishes, it's an advantage to refrigerate them overnight and remove the fat that congeals on the surface. With rare exception, these dishes also freeze beautifully. As a general rule, refrigerate for up to 4 days and freeze for up to 3 months.

Tips for Cooking on an Electric Stove

Because electric coils create such intense heat and respond so slowly to adjustments in temperature, here are a few thoughts to keep in mind:

- Make sure your cooker has a heavy, well-constructed bottom with a layer of copper or aluminum sandwiched between the stainless steel.

- If you experience scorching, use a Flame Tamer (page 4) to diffuse the heat.

- Lower the heat a minute or so before the cooker actually reaches high pressure to accommodate the time delay. Alternatively, after reaching high pressure, transfer the cooker to a burner preset to low (or whatever you've determined to be the correct setting for maintaining high pressure).

- Since I've tested all of the recipes in this book on a gas burner, make minor adjustments in the timing if necessary.

Adapting Favorite Recipes for the Pressure Cooker

If you'd like to prepare a favorite soup or stew in one-third the normal cooking time, here are some guidelines for adapting the recipe:

- Choose only those recipes that combine most of the ingredients at the beginning. Look for a similar dish in this book and loosely follow the procedure and timing. When in doubt, always err on the side of undercooking. Then finish the dish using standard stovetop cooking.

- As a general rule, reduce the liquid in soup and stew recipes by about 20 percent, since little or no liquid is lost during cooking.

- Increase the amount of herbs and spices by about 30 percent to accommodate for loss of intensity under pressure. Add some compatible chopped, fresh herbs at the end.

BASIC RECIPES

This chapter contains a selection of recipes you can use to enhance the flavor and bounty of one-pot meals. There are instructions for preparing pressure-cooked broths as well as suggestions for selecting tasty alternatives. I've also included recipes for making large quantities of beans, whole grains, white rice, polenta, and bulgur so that you can stock your freezer with cooked staples.

BROTHS UNDER PRESSURE

It's a breeze making all kinds of broths in the pressure cooker, and the brief time it takes to prepare a batch makes the pleasure of using homemade broths a realistic alternative to using canned and powdered versions.

I am using the word **broth** rather than **stock** because these recipes produce a lighter result than classic time-consuming preparations that require first roasting the ingredients and then simmering them for hours on end. You will be quite pleased with the good taste and excellent body of these quickly made broths. The pressure cooker is remarkably good at extracting flavor from the aromatic vegetables and gelatin from the bones. (Those who wish to take the extra step of roasting the ingredients before pressure cooking will find instructions in the 1997 edition of *The All New Joy of Cooking* and other basic cookbooks.)

All of the broth recipes were tested in a 6-quart cooker. If using an 8-quart model, you may increase the ingredients by about 30 percent.

General Tips

It's ideal to prepare beef, veal, and poultry broths a day in advance so that you can easily remove the fat that congeals on top after overnight refrigeration.

For maximum versatility, keep the broths salt-free. That way, if you are cooking beans in the broth, you won't have any concerns that they won't cook properly. (Salt can harden bean skins, preventing proper absorption of water.) All of the recipes are based on salt-free broth; if you use canned broths, see the section below on alternatives to homemade broth.

For a more intense broth, add only enough water to cover the ingredients rather than the amount recommended in the recipe. To concentrate the flavor after cooking, strain the broth and then boil the liquid vigorously over high heat until it is reduced to the desired concentration.

CAUTION: NO BACTERIA PLEASE!

Warm broth is an ideal breeding ground for bacteria. If you are not going to cook with the broth immediately, follow these guidelines to prevent the growth of bacteria:

Strain the finished broth as soon as the steam coming off the top has subsided. Pour the broth into storage containers of convenient sizes—perhaps one of 4-cup capacity, one of 2-cup, and the remainder of 1-cup—and set the uncovered containers on a large rack (like the ones used for cooling cookies) submerged in a sink filled with enough cold water to reach halfway up the sides of the containers. Add a tray of ice cubes to the water. After about a half hour, cover the containers and transfer them to the refrigerator. The next morning, remove the fat congealed on the surface. Date any containers you plan to store. Refrigerate the broth for a maximum of 3 days or freeze for up to 3 months.

When it comes time to use frozen broth, to avoid bacterial growth, defrost portions in a microwave or saucepan—or simply add a premeasured amount of frozen broth directly to the cooker. Do not defrost broth in the refrigerator or at room temperature.

Alternatives to Homemade Broth

Always purchase low-sodium versions. If you are cooking beans in a salted broth, dilute it by 50 percent with water to insure proper cooking, and reduce the amount of added salt suggested in the recipe.

Here are a few healthy, good-tasting alternatives to canned broths and bouillon cubes, which usually are high in sodium and contain MSG, artificial flavors, and other highly refined ingredients. I've included phone numbers in case you need help locating a source for these products.

Perfect Addition (714-640-0220): Good-quality frozen beef, fish, veal, vegetable, and chicken broths in concentrated form.

Pacific (503-692-9666): Free-range chicken broth packaged in 1-liter aseptic "bricks;" this company also makes an organic vegetable broth, but I do not care for the taste.

Vogue Vege Base (888-236-4144): Makes one of the better-tasting powdered vegetable broth bases.

BEEF BROTH

The pressure cooker produces a beef broth with considerable body because it makes such quick work of extracting the gelatin from the bones. Taking the time to first brown the beef deepens the flavor of this broth.

If you like, use a combination of shanks and oxtails and throw in some extra bones if you have any in the freezer. Sample the cooked meat, and if you think it has sufficient taste, use it for making hash.

1 HOUR HIGH PRESSURE

2 tablespoons vegetable oil

3 pounds bone-in meaty beef shanks (shins), or 2 pounds shanks and 1 pound oxtails, cut into 2-inch pieces (approximately) and well trimmed

8 cups cold water

2 large carrots, scrubbed or peeled and cut into chunks

2 large ribs celery, cut into chunks

2 large onions, peeled and quartered, or 1 large onion plus 4 or 5 leek greens

2 large bay leaves

Small bunch parsley stems

1/2 teaspoon dried thyme leaves

1/4 teaspoon whole black peppercorns

Over medium-high heat, heat 1 tablespoon of the oil in the cooker. Brown the beef in 2 or 3 batches, about 3 minutes on each side, taking care not to crowd the cooker. Add extra oil as needed. When the beef is browned, remove the last batch of beef from the cooker and tip off any excess fat.

Add 2 cups of the water and begin bringing to a boil over high heat as you stir to scrape up any browned bits of beef stuck to the bottom of the cooker. Add the remaining water, browned beef, and remaining ingredients. Once the water has come to a boil, skim off any foam that rises to the top. (Just get most of it; don't feel that you need to remove every last speck.) If the ingredients exceed the maximum recommended capacity, ladle off a bit of the water.

Lock the lid in place. Over high heat, bring the cooker to high pressure. Reduce the heat just enough to maintain high pressure and cook for 1 hour. If time permits, allow all or some of the pressure to come down naturally. Otherwise, quick-release the pressure by setting the cooker under cold running water. Remove the lid, tilting it away from you to allow excess steam to escape.

Allow the stock to cool slightly. Strain into storage containers, pressing the shanks and vegetables to release all of their liquid. Discard the solid ingredients (or reserve the meat for hash). To prevent bacterial growth, cool the broth rapidly and store as directed on page 13.

MAKES ABOUT 2 QUARTS

TURKEY BROTH

Turkey drumsticks and thighs create a marvelous, richly flavored broth with the added bonus of cooked turkey meat available for a salad, sandwich, or soup. Now that turkey parts are widely available, it's no longer necessary to wait until after Thanksgiving to prepare this broth. If you don't find turkey parts among the fresh meats in your supermarket, look for them in the freezer section. (For instructions on making the broth with a turkey carcass, see the variation on page 17.)

For many soups and stews, I've come to prefer the hearty flavor of turkey broth to the lighter taste of chicken broth. When you find turkey parts on sale, they are about one-third the price of chicken, making this broth a real bargain to prepare. In addition, since turkey is bred even leaner than chicken, there is little to no fat to skim off.

Try to find young turkey drumsticks (about 1 pound each) which will fit horizontally in the cooker, totally submerged in the water. For larger drumsticks, you can allow the bony ends to rest out of the liquid, near the upper rim of the cooker; just take care that they don't block the vent in the lid. You can use fresh or still-frozen parts in this recipe.

30 TO 40 MINUTES HIGH PRESSURE PLUS 10- TO 15-MINUTE NATURAL PRESSURE RELEASE

8 to 10 cups cold water

2 to 2½ pounds turkey drumsticks or drumsticks and thighs, skinned (see Tip)

1 large onion, peeled and cut into eighths

A few leek greens (optional)

3 large ribs celery, cut into 1-inch slices

2 large carrots, scrubbed or peeled and cut into 1-inch slices

2 large bay leaves

10 whole black peppercorns

Small bunch parsley stems (optional)

Pour 8 cups of water into the cooker and begin bringing to a boil over high heat. Set the drumsticks and/or thighs in the water, fleshy side down, then add the remaining ingredients. Add more water if you can without exceeding the maximum capacity advised by the manufacturer.

Lock the lid in place. Over high heat bring to high pressure. Reduce the heat just enough to maintain high pressure and cook for 30 minutes for fresh parts or 40 minutes for frozen parts. Allow the pressure to come down naturally, 10 to 15 minutes. Remove the lid, tilting it away from you to allow excess steam to escape.

Allow the stock to cool slightly. Strain into storage containers, pressing the turkey and vegetables to release all of their liquid. Discard the vegetables and reserve the turkey for use. To prevent bacterial growth, cool the broth rapidly and store as directed on page 13.

MAKES ABOUT 2½ QUARTS

TIP

Pull the skin and any fat down toward the bony part of the drumstick. Snip the skin off with a kitchen shears. (You probably won't need the shears when skinning the thighs.) If you'll have time to refrigerate the broth and remove any congealed fat, you don't have to bother skinning the pieces.

TURKEY CARCASS AND GIBLET BROTH

Here's how you make broth from the leftover carcass of a roasted turkey: Omit the fresh turkey drumsticks and thighs. Add the neck, giblets (but not the liver), vegetables, and seasonings. Loosely pack in the broken, cooked carcass and other bones until the cooker is a little more than two-thirds full. Add just enough water to cover. Proceed as directed in the recipe.

CHICKEN BROTH

Flavor-packed old stewing hens are few and far between, but since the pressure cooker is so good at extracting every last bit of flavor from meat and bones, you'll get a tasty, gelatinous broth even when using young broiler parts. For optimum flavor, use parts from a kosher or free-range chicken. If you'd like to prepare the broth from a whole chicken and reserve the meat for a salad or sandwiches, see the variation on page 19.

30 MINUTES HIGH PRESSURE

3 pounds chicken wings, backs, bones, and necks, rinsed

8 cups cold water

2 large carrots, scrubbed or peeled and chopped

2 large ribs celery, cut into 1-inch slices

2 large onions, peeled and quartered

Small bunch parsley stems

2 large bay leaves

¼ teaspoon whole black peppercorns

Place the chicken and water in the cooker and begin bringing to a boil over medium-high heat as you prepare and add the remaining ingredients. With a skimmer or large spoon, remove and discard any froth that rises to the surface. (Just get most of it; don't feel that you need to remove every last speck.)

Lock the lid in place. Over high heat, bring to high pressure. Lower the heat just enough to maintain high pressure and cook for 30 minutes. If time permits, let the pressure drop naturally, about 20 minutes. Otherwise quick-release the pressure by setting the cooker under cold running water.

Remove the lid, tilting it away from you to allow any excess steam to escape. Allow the stock to cool slightly. Strain into storage containers, pressing the chicken and vegetables to release all of their liquid. Discard the solid ingredients. To prevent bacterial growth, cool the broth rapidly and store as directed on page 13.

MAKES ABOUT 2 QUARTS

WHOLE CHICKEN BROTH

Omit the parts and substitute a 3-pound chicken cut into pieces and skinned. Proceed as directed and cook for 12 minutes under high pressure. Quick-release the pressure by setting the cooker under cold running water. With a slotted spoon, remove the cooked chicken (except for the wings, neck and back). When the parts are cool enough to handle, remove the meat and reserve for use. Return the bones to the cooker and return to high pressure for 18 more minutes. Proceed as directed.

VEAL BROTH

Omit the chicken and substitute 3 pounds of meaty veal neck bones. Cook for 45 minutes under pressure and proceed as directed.

VEGETABLE BROTH

After years of experimenting, I have come to the conclusion that it's worth a bit of extra time and effort to soften the vegetables in a tablespoon of butter or oil before adding the water and bringing the mixture up to pressure. This initial cooking draws out the vegetables' sweetness and results in a richer, more complex broth than one that is entirely fat-free. Broth made with a bit of fat also holds its flavor better when frozen. For optimum taste, always use vegetables that are crisp and fresh. Including a handful of lentils or split peas adds both flavor and body.

Since it takes as much time to soften the vegetables as it does to cook them under pressure—about 10 minutes—I speed up the process by cooking the onion while I chop the carrots and celery, adding these and the remaining ingredients as they're ready, and stirring every minute or so.

10 MINUTES HIGH PRESSURE

1 tablespoon butter or olive oil
1 large onion, peeled and coarsely chopped
3 large carrots, scrubbed or peeled and coarsely chopped
4 large ribs celery, coarsely chopped
6 cloves garlic, peeled and smashed
A few leek greens, coarsely chopped (optional)
11 to 12 cups water
Peels from 1 well-scrubbed potato (optional)
⅓ cup red lentils or split peas, rinsed and drained
Generous handful dried mushrooms
Small bunch parsley stems (optional)
2 large bay leaves

Over medium heat, heat the butter in the cooker until it begins to foam. Add the onion and cook, stirring every minute or so, as you prepare and add the carrots, celery, garlic, and leek greens, if using. If brown spots begin to appear on the bottom of the cooker, reduce the heat to low.

Continue to cook and stir the vegetables until the onion is very soft, about 10 minutes total. (For a darker stock with deeper flavor, raise the heat to medium-high and cook until the onion is lightly browned, another few minutes.)

Add 11 cups of water, the potato peelings, if using, red lentils, mushrooms, parsley, if using, and bay leaves. Add 1 more cup of water if it will fit into the cooker without exceeding the manufacturer's maximum fill recommendation.

Lock the lid in place. Over high heat bring to high pressure. Lower the heat just enough to maintain high pressure and cook for 10 minutes. If time permits, let the pressure drop naturally, about 20 minutes. Otherwise, quick-release the pressure by setting the cooker under cold running water. Remove the lid, tilting it away from you to allow excess steam to escape.

Allow the stock to cool slightly. Strain into storage containers, pressing the vegetables to release all of their liquid. Discard the vegetables and bay leaves. To prevent bacterial growth, cool the broth rapidly and store as directed on page 13.

MAKES ABOUT 2½ QUARTS

ASIAN VEGETABLE BROTH

Use light sesame or peanut oil and dried shiitake mushrooms. Substitute a small bunch of trimmed scallions for the onion and chopped cilantro for the parsley. Omit the peppercorns and add 6 to 8 quarter-sized slices of fresh ginger and 3 pods of star anise, if you like. The flavor shift is subtle but pleasant and works well with any Asian-inspired recipe that calls for vegetable broth.

FISH BROTH

Fish bones are getting harder and harder to come by, but if you can get some from a neighborhood fishmonger or a fisherman friend, here's a simple stock to prepare. It's a messy job to clean and chop a fish frame, so if you're not experienced with the task, ask your source to do it.

For best results, stick with non-oily, white-fleshed fish heads and bones. To avoid bitter taste and cloudiness, make sure that all of the gills are removed and the parts are thoroughly rinsed.

8 MINUTES HIGH PRESSURE

3 pounds fish heads and bones, thoroughly rinsed
1 large onion, peeled and sliced
A few leek greens (optional)
2 large carrots, scrubbed or peeled and coarsely chopped
3 large ribs celery, coarsely chopped
2 large bay leaves
Small bunch parsley stems
8 whole black peppercorns
7 to 8 cups cold water

Cut the bones, if necessary, so that they will fit into the cooker. Place the fish heads and bones plus the vegetables, seasonings, and 7 cups of water in the cooker. Add the remaining cup of water if it fits without exceeding the maximum capacity advised by the manufacturer. Over medium heat, bring to a boil, skimming off any froth that rises to the surface.

Lock the lid in place. Over high heat bring to high pressure. Reduce the heat just enough to maintain high pressure and cook for 8 minutes. Quick-release the pressure. Remove the lid, tilting it away from you to allow excess steam to escape.

Allow the stock to cool slightly. Strain into storage containers and discard the solids. To prevent bacterial growth, cool the broth rapidly and store as directed on page 13.

MAKES ABOUT 1 ½ QUARTS

SHRIMP BROTH

This is a tasty alternative to fish broth when you have cleaned the shrimp your-self and want to make use of the flavorful peelings. For example, it's a fine broth to use if you're making the Shrimp Risotto on page 159.

If your fish market sells shrimp with their heads intact, by all means add the heads for an even more flavorful broth.

5 MINUTES HIGH PRESSURE

Peelings from 1 ¼ pounds shrimp (2½ to 3 cups)
1 medium onion, peeled and quartered
2 large ribs celery, coarsely chopped
Small bunch parsley stems
½ teaspoon whole black or white peppercorns
½ teaspoon whole coriander seeds
5 ½ cups cold water

Place all of the ingredients in the cooker. Lock the lid in place. Over high heat, bring to high pressure. Reduce the heat just enough to maintain high pressure and cook for 5 minutes. If time permits, allow the pressure to come down natu-rally, about 10 minutes. Otherwise, quick-release the pressure. Remove the lid, tilting it away from you to allow excess steam to escape.

Allow the stock to cool slightly. Strain into storage containers, pressing the veg-etables to release all of their liquid. Discard the solids. To prevent bacterial growth, cool the broth rapidly and store as directed on page 13.

MAKES ABOUT 5 ½ CUPS

BEANS UNDER PRESSURE

You can pressure-cook beans from scratch in about a quarter of the time it takes using standard cooking techniques. For example, presoaked pinto beans become tender in 6 minutes and chickpeas in 16. Because they are so nutritious, and bean cooking is one of the things that the pressure cooker does best, I've included beans in many of the recipes in this collection.

When practical, I call for unsoaked beans, but experience has revealed that presoaked beans cook more evenly and are usually easier on the digestive system. If you haven't planned in advance and presoaked the beans, try the speed-soak technique described below.

Lay-Away Beans

Cooking beans at home is an economical alternative to using canned beans, particularly when you cook a large batch in advance and refrigerate or freeze extra in premeasured portions. Cook a pound (about 2¼ cups dried beans) at a time and divide the beans into three zipper-topped plastic freezer bags, each containing about 1½ cups of cooked beans. Date the bags and, for optimum taste, use the frozen beans within 3 months. All of the recipes in this book that use already cooked beans call for 1½ cups so that you can use either home-cooked beans or a 15-ounce can of purchased beans interchangeably.

Selecting and Storing Beans

Although dried beans remain edible indefinitely, they do not age well! Indeed, they lose flavor and moisture over time. If very old, some beans will never become tender no matter how long you cook them. For these reasons, it's best to purchase beans from stores where there is a good turnover—particularly when buying beans in bulk. Select beans whose skins are intact and brightly colored. Faded beans or those with chipped skins suggest improper harvesting or storage.

Once you have them at home, store the beans in a tightly sealed container in a cool, dark place. Aim to cook them within 6 months.

Speed-Soaking Beans

The pressure cooker offers the option of speed-soaking, a technique that takes about 20 minutes and is roughly equivalent to soaking overnight. This method is not completely reliable: If the beans are very fresh, they sometimes begin to cook. (This is more a consideration with small beans than with large ones.) However, the method is handy for a last-minute presoak:

- Place the water and beans in the cooker, in a ratio of 3 parts water to 1 part beans. (If using an old-fashioned jiggle-top cooker and preparing a large quantity of beans, add 2 teaspoons of oil per cup of dried beans to control the foam that develops during speed soaking.)

- Lock the lid in place. Over high heat, bring to high pressure.

- **For small beans,** such as navies: As soon as high pressure is reached, turn off the heat.

- **For medium beans,** such as Great Northerns: Cook for 1 minute under high pressure.

- **For large beans,** such as chickpeas: Cook for 3 minutes under high pressure.

- Turn off the heat and allow the pressure to come down naturally. Remove the lid, tilting it away from you to allow excess steam to escape.

- Drain and rinse beans and proceed as directed in the recipe.

Storing Soaked Beans

If your plans change and you don't have time to cook beans after you've soaked them, drain and refrigerate them for up to 2 days or freeze for up to 2 months. Defrost them before cooking. Soaked beans that have been frozen take about 10 percent less time to cook and don't hold their shape well. They are best used in soups, dips, or purees.

The Canned Bean Alternative

I always keep a range of canned beans on hand for spontaneous meals and for pressure-cooker recipes that call for already cooked beans. I use Eden brand organic canned beans and find their flavor and texture remarkably close to home-cooked. If using standard supermarket varieties, be sure to drain off the canning liquid and rinse the beans thoroughly to wash away excessive saltiness. If using organic beans, there's no need to rinse, and you can use the canning liquid to replace an equal amount of water or broth.

BASIC RECIPE FOR BEANS

Since an overcooked bean is mushy and has diminished flavor, pressure-cook beans until they are just short of done. When time permits, let the pressure come down naturally, a more gentle approach than using the vigorous quick-release, which causes much turbulence in the cooker and is likely to burst the beans' skins. (When timing beans, keep in mind that a 10-minute natural pressure release is roughly equivalent to 4 minutes of cooking under pressure.) If more cooking is required, simmer the beans in the standard way, with the lid ajar, until they are tender.

Here are some general rules for pressure-cooking beans:

■ Use 3 cups of water or unsalted broth for each cup of dried beans. Do not fill the cooker more than halfway.

■ Add 2 teaspoons of oil for every cup of dried beans. The oil is required to prevent foaming that might catapult a bean skin into the vent and block the release of excess pressure.

■ If you wish, add a large onion, quartered, a few cloves garlic, and 2 large bay leaves. Do not add salt, which retards cooking by hardening the bean skins.

■ Lock the lid in place and over high heat bring to high pressure.

■ **For large (soaked) beans,** such as chickpeas, black soy beans, and favas: Cook for 10 minutes under pressure.

■ **For medium (soaked) beans,** such as black beans, cannellinis, Great Northerns, and red kidneys: Cook for 3 minutes under pressure.

■ **For small (soaked) beans,** such as navies, adzukis, baby limas, and pintos: Cook for 2 minutes under pressure.

■ Allow the pressure to come down naturally.

■ If the beans are not sufficiently tender, set the lid slightly ajar and simmer at a gentle boil over low to medium heat until done.

■ Drain the beans. (If you like the way the liquid tastes, reserve it for soup or grain cooking.) Remove and discard the vegetables and bay leaves, if used. Use immediately, refrigerate in a sealed container for up to 3 days, or let cool completely before dividing into portions and storing as described in Lay-Away Beans, page 24.

GRAINS UNDER PRESSURE

Eating whole grains such as brown rice or wheat berries on a regular basis becomes more feasible when you can cook them in 15 minutes rather than an hour or more. Whole grains are rich in nutrients and high in fiber, and once you get used to having them in your diet, their delightful chewiness becomes addictive.

I've recently discovered that whole grains tenderize considerably more quickly when cooked in an abundance of water—much like pasta—rather than when prepared pilaf-style with limited liquid. As an added bonus, this simple approach eliminates any possibility that the grains will absorb all of the liquid and stick to the bottom of the pot.

While writing this one-pot-meal book, I experimented with duplex cooking: setting grains and water in a heatproof bowl that floated on top of a stew so that both stew and grains would cook simultaneously. When this technique worked it was splendidly efficient, but results were not sufficiently reliable to set forth a formula here.

However, since it's ideal to serve many of the stews in this collection over grains or rice, I came up with a system for pressure-cooking a large batch of whole grains in advance, then freezing them for later use. For details, see Lay-Away Grains, below. For a similar system using white rice—what I call "Ready Rice"—see page 31.

Lay-Away Grains

I know it's hard to believe, but cooked whole grains that are frozen and then defrosted in the microwave taste just about as good as a freshly made batch. It's therefore quite efficient to cook more than you need and freeze the remainder in convenient portion sizes in dated, zipper-topped, plastic freezer bags. Cooked whole grains can be frozen for up to 3 months. The grains tend to freeze in a block. If you don't need the whole bagful, bang the grains against the kitchen counter to loosen the amount you need. Frozen grains may be added directly to cooked soups or stews and heated until they become plump and soft, about 3 minutes.

Alternatively, if you wish to serve a bed of grains under a stew, set the frozen grains in a bowl, place a sheet of waxed paper or paper towel loosely on top, and microwave on high, stirring once or twice, until the grains are hot and rehydrated, 1 to 4 minutes, depending on the quantity and type of grain. If you don't own a microwave, defrost and rehydrate the cooked grains by placing them in a steamer basket over boiling water in a covered pot and steam until ready to eat, about 5 minutes.

You may use these same techniques to rehydrate grains that have become dried out after a sojourn in the refrigerator.

Selecting and Storing Grains

Whole grains still have their oil-packed germ intact and can quickly go rancid if not properly stored. Your best bet is to purchase grains vacuum-sealed in plastic bags. If you prefer to buy grains from the bulk bin, make sure they smell sweet and have no hint of a musky odor.

Once at home, freeze the grains in a zipper-topped plastic freezer bag for up to 6 months.

WHOLE GRAIN COOKING CHART

CUPS GRAIN	CUPS WATER	TABLESPOONS OIL	TEASPOONS SALT (OPTIONAL)	APPROXIMATE YIELD IN CUPS
1	4	1	½	2
2	7	1½	¾	4½
3	9	1½	1	7

Note: When cooking pearl or pot barley, double the amount of oil to control foaming. The yield will be 30 percent more.

TIMING FOR WHOLE GRAINS

15 MINUTES	18 MINUTES	22 MINUTES
brown rice (short- and long-grain)	kamut	wild rice
pearl barley	pot barley	
black barley	rye	
whole oats	spelt	
	wheat berries	

BASIC RECIPE FOR WHOLE GRAINS

This recipe is set up so that you can prepare 7 cups of cooked whole grains with the idea of freezing the leftovers for future meals (see Lay-Away Grains, page 27). If you wish to prepare a smaller quantity, just consult the chart on page 28 for proportions of grain and water and follow the same instructions.

15 TO 22 MINUTES HIGH PRESSURE (DEPENDING UPON TYPE OF GRAIN)

3 cups whole grains, rinsed and drained

9 cups water

1 1/2 tablespoons taste-free vegetable oil, such as canola (see Tips)

1 teaspoon salt (optional)

Place the ingredients in the cooker.

Lock the lid in place. Over high heat, bring to high pressure. Lower the heat just enough to maintain high pressure and cook according to the time indicated in the table on page 28.

Quick-release the pressure by placing the cooker under cold running water. (Do not use a stovetop quick-release method, which is likely to result in sputtering at the vent.) Remove the lid, tilting it away from you to allow any excess steam to escape.

If the grains are not sufficiently tender—remember that whole grains are always a bit chewy—replace (but do not lock) the lid and simmer over medium heat until done.

Drain thoroughly. (If you like the way the liquid tastes, reserve it for use as the base for soups or broths.) For fluffier, drier grains, immediately return the hot grains to the cooker, set the lid in place, and let steam in the residual heat for 5 minutes. Fluff up the grains before serving.

MAKES ABOUT 7 CUPS

TIPS

Here are a few points to keep in mind when cooking whole grains under pressure:

■ To subdue the foaming action characteristic of grain cooking, always add at least a tablespoon of oil. The oil prevents the grains from being catapulted into the vent, where they might block the release of excess pressure.

■ Do not fill the cooker beyond halfway. In a 6-quart cooker, you can cook 3 cups of dry grain in 9 cups of water—but no more.

■ Grains with the same cooking time may be prepared together. (A favorite combination is brown rice and black barley.) Or you may simply cook a variety of grains and use the longest cooking time required by one or more of them. (For example, cook wild rice and wheat berries together for 22 minutes.) With the exception of oats, whole grains remain fairly chewy, so overcooking is rarely an issue.

■ Release pressure by setting the cooker under cold running water to avoid sputtering at the vent.

■ Clean the lid, pressure mechanism, and vent thoroughly after cooking grains.

READY RICE

Like Lay-Away Grains, this approach involves cooking a large quantity of white rice under pressure, then freezing it in portion sizes. Since cooking white rice from scratch takes only about 20 minutes by conventional methods, you may prefer to prepare a fresh batch alongside your pressure-cooked one-pot, but try this handy technique if that seems too much of a bother. You can also use these instructions for preparing smaller quantities of white rice; consult the chart on page 32 for proportions.

3 MINUTES HIGH PRESSURE PLUS 7-MINUTE NATURAL PRESSURE RELEASE

4 ¼ cups water

1 ½ teaspoons salt

3 cups extra-long-grain or basmati white rice

Over high heat, bring the water and salt to a boil in the cooker. Stir in the rice.

Lock the lid in place. Over high heat, bring to high pressure. Reduce the heat just enough to maintain high pressure and cook for 3 minutes. Allow the pressure to come down naturally for 7 minutes. Quick-release any remaining pressure. Remove the lid, tilting it away from you to allow excess steam to escape.

Fluff up the rice. Use immediately or allow the rice to cool to room temperature and freeze in convenient portion sizes according to instructions in Lay-Away Grains on page 27. Add frozen to cooked soups or stews or defrost and reheat as directed in that section.

MAKES 7 ½ TO 8 CUPS

RICE TIMBALES

Instead of serving chili and other stews over a bed of rice, try this alternative: Lightly coat a small custard cup or individual soufflé dish with pan spray or brush it with oil. Gently press a single portion of freshly cooked white rice into the cup. Turn the cup upside down onto the center of each plate and gently lift it off. Surround each rice timbale with stew and garnish with chopped fresh herbs.

WHITE RICE COOKING CHART

CUPS WHITE BASMATI OR EXTRA-LONG-GRAIN WHITE RICE	CUPS LIQUID	TEASPOONS SALT (OPTIONAL)	YIELD IN CUPS
1	1½	½	3
1½	2¼	¾	4–4½
2	3	1	5½–6
3	4¼	1½	7½–8

POLENTA PRESTO

In recent years, an excellent "quick-cooking" polenta has become more available. I've used Valsugana and Tipiak brands with excellent results. The polenta cooks in 5 minutes or less, making it a handy, last-minute alternative to rice or pasta. Many of the stews in this book, particularly those inspired by the recipes of Italy and Mexico, are especially delicious when ladled over polenta.

Follow the package instructions to make as much as you like. To enhance flavor, stir in one or more of the following, just before serving: A bit of roasted garlic–flavored olive oil, butter, chopped fresh herbs, or grated Parmesan cheese.

You can serve the polenta in a mound when it's still soft and porridge-like. Alternatively, pour the piping-hot cooked polenta into a pie plate, smooth off the top with a spatula, and let it firm up as it cools, which takes about 15 minutes. Use the polenta immediately or refrigerate for up to 5 days, and cut into wedges as needed. Then reheat in the microwave or pan-fry in a little olive oil.

Wedges of cooked polenta freeze well when doused with a liberal portion of a soupy stew, such as Sicilian Chicken with Olives and Escarole. To serve, just defrost and heat in the microwave. I don't recommend freezing cooked polenta on its own: The taste and texture aren't sufficiently appealing.

BASIC BULGUR

Coarse bulgur makes a hearty and appealing alternative to couscous and goes very well with Middle Eastern dishes. Using the simple technique described below, steep the bulgur in a heatproof casserole, and if the grain is not quite tender, finish it off for a minute or two in the microwave.

I'm including basic instructions here because coarse bulgur is sold either in bulk or in packages that don't include cooking instructions. You can find coarse bulgur in most health-food stores or packaged under the Goya label in the Hispanic section of some supermarkets. For more information on coarse bulgur, check the Guide to Ingredients, page 234.

Cooked bulgur freezes very well; you may wish to double this recipe and use the Lay-Away plan described on page 27.

1 cup coarse bulgur
2 cups boiling water

Set the bulgur in a microwave-friendly bowl. Pour the boiling water on top and quickly stir. Cover tightly with plastic wrap and let steep until the bulgur is tender and the water has been absorbed, about 20 minutes.

After 20 minutes, if the bulgur isn't quite tender, stir in 2 tablespoons of water and create a narrow vent by folding back one side of the plastic wrap. Microwave on high for 1 minute. Let stand for 1 minute. Repeat this process, if necessary, until all of the liquid has been absorbed and the grains are tender.

Fluff up and serve or cool to room temperature and refrigerate or freeze for later use. Before serving, microwave according to the directions in Lay-Away Grains (page 27).

MAKES 3½ CUPS

ONE-POT MEALS IN MINUTES

Although most of the recipes in this book fall into the quick and easy category, I've singled out the ones listed below because they require relatively little preparation time or very brief cooking—or both. You can have all of these dishes on the table within thirty minutes of entering the kitchen. After you've made the recipe once, things will go even faster.

TEN OF THE QUICKEST RECIPES

Quick Curried Rice with Chicken, page 78

Chicken and Spinach in Curried Pasta Sauce, page 88

Split Pea Soup with Smoked Turkey, page 91

Cabbage and Potato Soup with Sweet Italian Sausage, page 102

Tamed Pork Vindaloo with Spinach and Potatoes, page 114

Lamb with Apricots, Prunes, and Mint, page 132

Veal with Olives and Artichoke Hearts, page 146

Scrod and Corn Chowder, page 158

Potato-Cauliflower Curry with Mango Yogurt, page 206

Risotto with Green Peas, page 219

BEEF

BEEF UNDER PRESSURE

One major aspect of cooking beef under pressure sets it apart from other meats: You must allow the pressure to come down naturally when cooking pieces larger than ½ inch thick. If you use a quick-release method, the meat seizes up and becomes tough. This is not as true of the fattier cuts—such as short ribs or brisket—but I don't take a chance even with those.

As long as you keep that rule in mind (the recipes will always remind you!), pressure-cooking beef is quite straightforward. Here are a few tips to guarantee your success:

In his informative *Meat Book*, butcher Jack Ubaldi advises selecting beef with bright color and delicate lines of fat (marbling) throughout. With the exception of ground meat, which is quite perishable and should be cooked as soon as possible, beef may be refrigerated until the expiration date or up to five days, whichever is sooner.

Avoid buying cubed beef labeled "stew meat." Such a package is likely to contain leftover odds and ends from different parts of the animal, and they probably won't cook evenly. Choose instead a boneless chuck roast and cube it at home. Chuck roast has a dizzying variety of names, including shoulder roast, shoulder clod roast, boneless arm pot roast, blade roast, or cross rib roast. If in doubt, ask the butcher or a knowledgeable local cook.

If you can't find a whole roast, buy a chuck steak (preferably boneless) about 1-inch thick and cut it up yourself. Count on loosing more than 30 percent of the weight when you trim off the fat, gristle, and bones. Always include the bones in the stew for added flavor.

When buying beef, USDA gradings can be quite confusing. It helps to remember that "choice is a good choice." Choice meat is grainy and marbled with fat (albeit unevenly) so that it remains moist during cooking. If "top choice" is available, opt for that rather than "choice."

ITALIAN WEDDING SOUP

My first taste of Italian wedding soup was in a small-town restaurant in Pennsylvania. I'd never heard of this dish before, but my significant other spoke of it with great nostalgia, recalling how Italian neighbors in the Bronx served it on special occasions during his childhood.

The restaurant version was so-so, but I could tell that the soup had great potential. So here you have it: a traditionally long-simmered soup made with meatballs, escarole, and little star-shaped pastina, cooked in a flash under pressure. For optimum results, make the little meatballs bite-sized and use homemade broth. If you like smoothly textured meatballs, prepare them with a food processor or mixer rather than by hand.

1 MINUTE HIGH PRESSURE

MEATBALLS
¾ pound ground beef

2 tablespoons freshly grated Pecorino Romano or Parmesan cheese

1 large egg

1 teaspoon dried oregano leaves

1 teaspoon granulated or powdered garlic, or 1 ½ teaspoons minced fresh garlic

½ teaspoon salt

⅛ teaspoon freshly ground black pepper

SOUP
1 tablespoon olive oil

2 cups thinly sliced leeks or coarsely chopped onions

4 tablespoons tomato paste

8 cups chicken or beef broth (or better yet, a combination)

1 tablespoon Italian herb blend (page 238 or store-bought)

3 large carrots, peeled, halved lengthwise, and cut into ½-inch slices

½ cup pastini or other small pasta, such as tubetti or ditalini

1 ½ pounds escarole, trimmed and coarsely chopped

1 cup freshly grated Pecorino Romano or Parmesan cheese

In a large bowl, combine the ingredients for the meatballs by blending them with your hands. Shape the mixture into bite-sized balls, each a little smaller than ½ inch in diameter. Set aside.

For the soup, heat the oil in the cooker over medium-high heat. Cook the leeks, stirring frequently, for 2 minutes. Blend in the tomato paste and cook for an additional minute, stirring constantly. Add the broth and herbs, taking care to scrape up any browned bits sticking to the bottom of the cooker. Add the carrots. Over high heat, bring to a boil.

When the broth is boiling, add the pastini. Lower the heat to medium. Then gently drop the meatballs into the broth a few at a time. Set the escarole on top. (Don't be concerned that the cooker will be filled almost to the brim; the escarole will shrink dramatically as the cooker comes up to pressure.)

Lock the lid in place. Over high heat, bring to high pressure. (This may take as long as 5 minutes since the cooker is so full.) Reduce the heat just enough to maintain high pressure and cook for 1 minute. Quick-release the pressure by setting the cooker under cold running water.

Stir gently. With a slotted spoon, remove one meatball. Slice it in half and check that it is cooked throughout. If not, simmer the broth, uncovered, over medium heat until the meatballs are done, 1 to 2 minutes more.

Adjust the seasonings and serve in large bowls. Top each portion with a generous sprinkling of grated cheese. Pass the remaining cheese in a small bowl.

SERVES 6

BEEF, MUSHROOM, AND BARLEY SOUP

Flavor echoes of Eastern Europe and the soothing texture of barley create a comforting soup guaranteed to warm you on a cold winter's night. Split peas give substance to the flavorful broth, and frozen peas stirred in at the end add cheerful pops of color. Dill-flecked sour cream gives the soup a rich finish. Use fresh dill, if you can, for its vibrant color and flavor.

This soup thickens on standing because the barley continues to absorb liquid. Thin it with broth, if you wish, or consider it a stew.

20 MINUTES HIGH PRESSURE

1 MINUTE ADDITIONAL COOKING

1 ounce (about 1 cup loosely packed) dried mushrooms

3 cups boiling water

1/2 cup sour cream

1/4 cup finely chopped fresh dill or 1 teaspoon dried, or more to taste

1 tablespoon butter or vegetable oil

2 cups coarsely chopped onions

1 pound boneless beef chuck, cut into 1/2-inch cubes, well trimmed

3 cups chicken or turkey broth

4 large ribs celery, cut into 1/2-inch slices

3 small parsnips or medium carrots or a mixture, peeled and cut into 1-inch chunks (about 2 1/2 cups)

1/2 cup pearl barley, rinsed and drained

1/2 cup green split peas, picked over and rinsed

2 large bay leaves

1 teaspoon salt, or to taste

Freshly ground black pepper

1 to 2 tablespoons freshly squeezed lemon juice (optional)

1 cup frozen green peas (rinse away any ice crystals)

Set the dried mushrooms in a bowl or 1-quart glass measuring cup and pour the boiling water on top. Cover with a plate and set aside to steep until soft, about 10 minutes. Meanwhile, in a medium bowl, combine the sour cream and dill.

Cover and set aside, or refrigerate if you are not planning to serve the soup right after it's cooked.

Heat the butter in the cooker over medium-high heat until it begins to foam. Add the onions and cook, stirring frequently, for 2 minutes. Add the chuck and continue cooking, stirring frequently, until the meat turns from red to brown, 2 to 3 minutes more. Add the broth and take care to scrape up any browned bits stuck to the bottom of the cooker. Begin bringing to a boil.

Lift the softened mushrooms out of the soaking water with a slotted spoon. Chop coarsely, then add the mushrooms to the pot. Gently pour the mushroom broth into the cooker, leaving behind any sandy residue on the bottom of the bowl. Add the celery, parsnips, barley, split peas, bay leaves, salt, and pepper.

Lock the lid in place. Over high heat, bring to high pressure. Lower the heat to maintain high pressure and cook for 20 minutes. If time permits, let the pressure drop naturally. Otherwise, quick-release the pressure by setting the cooker under cold running water. Remove the lid, tilting it away from you to allow excess steam to escape.

Stir well and remove the bay leaves. Ladle out about a cup of liquid and whisk it into the sour cream–dill combination. Vigorously stir this mixture back into the pot until it is well blended. Adjust the seasonings, adding more dill, salt, and pepper, if needed. Add a bit of lemon juice if you'd like to sharpen the flavors. Add the frozen green peas and cook until they are tender-crisp, about 1 minute. Serve the soup in large bowls.

SERVES 6

BEEF AND BEAN CHILI WITH ROASTED RED PEPPERS

There are probably as many versions of chili as there are cooks who make it. My special touches include using small pieces of beef instead of ground, and enhancing commercial chili powder by adding cinnamon, some extra cumin and oregano, and two chipotle chiles. Chipotles are dried, smoked jalapeños, and they vary in heat from "just a little" to intense. Include a few of the chipotle seeds to guarantee an incendiary chili. (Wear rubber gloves when handling the chiles.)

For optimum taste, make sure that your chili powder is fresh and that you like its flavor. I recommend the Penzeys mail-order chili blend (page 245), which is made up primarily of ground mild ancho chiles. For a fire-alarm-hot chili, the Frontier brand sold in many health-food stores is a good choice.

Roasted red bell peppers stirred in at the end contribute striking color and texture, and a garnish of Cilantro-Lime Cream really brings this chili over the top.

If you're one of those folks who consider it sacrilege to include beans in your chili, have a look at the all-beef variation below. And if it's a vegetarian chili you're looking for, see page 176.

Serve the chili over rice or accompany it with warm tortillas or cornbread.

15 MINUTES HIGH PRESSURE

3 MINUTES ADDITIONAL COOKING

1 cup red kidney beans, picked over and rinsed, soaked overnight in ample water to cover or speed-soaked (page 24)

2 tablespoons olive oil, or more if needed

1 1/2 pounds boneless beef chuck, cut into 1/2-inch pieces, well trimmed

2 cups coarsely chopped onions

2 teaspoons whole cumin seeds

2 tablespoons mild chili powder, or more to taste

2 cups beef, chicken, or turkey broth

1 large green bell pepper, seeded and diced

Scant 1/4 teaspoon ground cinnamon

2 dried chipotle chiles, stemmed, seeded, and snipped into bits, or ⅛ teaspoon cayenne

3 tablespoons tomato paste

2 large cloves garlic, pushed though a press

1 teaspoon dried oregano leaves

Salt and freshly ground black pepper to taste

2 large red bell peppers, roasted (page 241), seeded, and cut into ½-inch squares

1 tablespoon freshly squeezed lime juice, or more to taste

CILANTRO-LIME CREAM

1 cup sour cream

½ cup tightly packed chopped fresh cilantro

1 tablespoon freshly squeezed lime juice

¼ teaspoon salt, or more to taste

Drain the beans and set aside. Heat a tablespoon of the oil in the cooker over medium-high heat. Brown the beef in 3 batches, adding more oil if needed. Set aside the beef on a platter. Heat another tablespoon of oil, add the onions and cumin, and cook for 1 minute, stirring frequently. Return all of the beef to the cooker, add the chili powder, stir to coat the beef, and cook for an additional minute. Add the broth and stir well, taking care to scrape up any browned bits stuck to the bottom of the cooker. Stir in the reserved beans, green pepper, cinnamon, and chipotle.

Lock the lid in place. Over high heat, bring to high pressure. Lower the heat just enough to maintain high pressure and cook for 15 minutes. If time permits, allow the pressure to come down naturally; otherwise use a quick-release method. Remove the lid, tilting it away from you to allow any excess steam to escape. If the meat or beans are not sufficiently tender, return to high pressure for 5 minutes more, or cover and simmer over medium heat until done.

While the chili is cooking, combine the ingredients for the Cilantro-Lime Cream in a bowl and set aside in the refrigerator.

Blend the tomato paste into the chili. Add the garlic, oregano, salt and pepper. Stir in more chili powder, if needed. Simmer over medium heat until the flavors mingle and the garlic loses its raw taste, about 3 minutes.

continued

If the chili is too soupy, you may set it aside for a few hours at room temperature during which time it will thicken considerably. If using immediately, mash about ½ cup of beans against the side of the cooker and stir in.

Just before serving, stir in the roasted red peppers, and cook for another minute. Stir in enough lime juice to punch up the flavors. Garnish each portion with a generous dollop of Cilantro-Lime Cream and pass the remainder at the table.

SERVES 4 TO 6

NO-BEAN BEEF CHILI

Eliminate the kidney beans and increase the beef to 2 pounds. Cut the beef into 1-inch chunks and brown as directed. Proceed with the recipe, but reduce the broth to 1 cup. After adding the green pepper, cinnamon, and chipotle, pour one 15-ounce can drained diced tomatoes on top. *Do not stir.* Proceed with the recipe, but increase the cooking time to 20 minutes under pressure and let the pressure come down naturally. Omit the tomato paste. If the cooked chili is too thin, stir in 3 tablespoons (or more, if needed) masa harina, instant polenta, or cornmeal, and cook uncovered at a gentle boil over medium heat stirring frequently until the chili has thickened, about 3 minutes.

OLD-FASHIONED BEEF STEW

In this stew, you have both an American and a pressure-cooker classic. I have a few suggestions for making it come out perfect every time:

- *Buy a whole boneless beef chuck roast and cube it yourself, an easy task with a good chef's knife. This way, you'll be sure that all of the meat comes from the same part of the animal and will cook evenly. (For alternatives, see page 37.)*

- *Take the time to brown the meat properly (see page 10) to intensify its flavor.*

- *Add a little good-quality, dry red wine to deepen the flavor of the gravy.*

- *Cook the beef until it is meltingly tender.*

- *Thicken the gravy without added flour or fat by mashing a few pieces of cooked potato against the sides of the cooker, then stirring in.*

Since potatoes don't freeze very well, if you're planning to freeze a portion of this stew, cook only the amount of potatoes you'll need right away. Then cook up a fresh batch of potatoes as directed in broth or water before heating up the defrosted stew.

30 MINUTES HIGH PRESSURE PLUS 15-MINUTE NATURAL PRESSURE RELEASE (BEEF)

5 MINUTES HIGH PRESSURE (VEGETABLES)

1 TO 2 MINUTES ADDITIONAL COOKING

2 to 3 tablespoons vegetable oil
3 pounds boneless beef chuck roast, cut into 1-inch pieces, well trimmed
2 cups coarsely chopped onions
3 tablespoons tomato paste
⅓ cup dry red wine (optional)
1¾ cups beef, chicken, or turkey broth
1 tablespoon Worcestershire sauce
2 large bay leaves

continued

½ teaspoon salt, or to taste

1 large clove garlic, pushed through a press

1 teaspoon dried thyme leaves, or more to taste

⅛ teaspoon ground allspice, or more to taste

Freshly ground black pepper to taste

3 pounds Yukon Gold potatoes, peeled and cut into 1½-inch chunks

1 pound carrots, peeled and cut into 2-inch chunks, or ready-to-eat baby carrots

One 10-ounce package frozen green peas (rinse away any ice crystals)

⅓ cup chopped fresh parsley, for garnish

Over medium-high heat, heat 1 tablespoon of oil in the cooker. Brown the beef in 4 batches, stirring frequently to prevent sticking, about 4 minutes per batch. Add extra oil as needed. Set the browned beef aside.

Add another tablespoon of oil if needed, and cook the onions over medium-high heat for 1 minute. Stir in the tomato paste and cook for an additional minute, stirring constantly. Add the wine, if using, and cook until it evaporates, about 30 seconds. Add the broth and stir well to scrape up any browned bits sticking to the bottom of the cooker. Add the browned beef with accumulated juices, Worcestershire sauce, bay leaves, and salt.

Lock the lid in place. Over high heat, bring to high pressure. Reduce the heat just enough to maintain high pressure and cook for 30 minutes. Allow the pressure to come down naturally for 15 minutes. Remove the lid, tilting it away from you to allow excess steam to escape. If the beef is not sufficiently tender, return to high pressure for 5 minutes more. Again, let the pressure come down naturally.

With a slotted spoon, transfer the beef to a bowl. Discard the bay leaves. Stir in the garlic, thyme, allspice, pepper, and potatoes. Set the carrots on top. Lock the lid in place. Over high heat, bring to high pressure. Reduce the heat just enough to maintain high pressure and cook for 5 minutes. Quick-release the pressure. Remove the lid, tilting it away from you to allow excess steam to escape. If the vegetables are not sufficiently tender, set the lid in place and allow them to steam in the residual heat until done, another minute or two.

Set the cooker over medium heat and add more thyme and allspice, if needed. If you'd like to thicken the gravy, mash a few pieces of potato against the sides of the cooker with a fork, and stir the mash into the stew. Return the beef to the pot and stir in the green peas. Cook until the beef is good and hot and the peas are tender but still bright green, 1 to 2 minutes. Meanwhile, adjust for salt and pepper. Serve individual portions lightly garnished with parsley.

SERVES 6

BEEF STEW WITH TURNIPS

When cooking the vegetables, add 1 pound peeled purple-topped turnips, cut into 1-inch cubes. Set them on top of the carrots.

BEEF STEW WITH TOMATOES AND STRING BEANS

Substitute 1 teaspoon dried oregano for the allspice. Once the potatoes and carrots have been added, pour over one 15-ounce can diced tomatoes with liquid. *Do not stir.*

Instead of green peas, use 10 ounces fresh or frozen cut string beans. Cook the stew, covered, over medium heat, until they are tender, about 5 minutes. If you wish, garnish with chopped fresh basil instead of parsley.

CHUCK WAGON BEEF STEW WITH CHEDDAR-SMASHED POTATOES

Here's the meat-and-potatoes dish to make when you feel like getting on with it—no time lingering over browning the meat and no extra step for cooking the potatoes. This no-frills approach is all thanks to the ingenuity of cowboy cooks who never wasted a thing: When leftover morning coffee found its way into the dinner stew, they discovered that it deepened the flavors remarkably well. (Northern Italian cooks use a similar approach by adding espresso to a beef stew called stacotto al caffè.*) The sauce is thin, but memorably laced with the smoky scent of bacon. By the way, you won't actually taste the coffee. If you wish, you may substitute beef broth.*

In this recipe, the potatoes are cooked along with the beef right from the start. It's no problem if they get a bit overcooked since they are to be mashed coarsely with some sharp cheddar and crispy bacon bits. Serve them in a mound in the middle of the stew.

20 MINUTES HIGH PRESSURE PLUS 15-MINUTE NATURAL PRESSURE RELEASE

3 strips bacon, chopped

1½ cups coarsely chopped onions

1 cup strong black coffee or beef broth

2 tablespoons Worcestershire sauce

2½ pounds boneless beef chuck, cut into 1-inch cubes, well trimmed

2 large bay leaves

3 pounds Idaho or russet potatoes, scrubbed or peeled, then halved

1½ cups grated sharp cheddar or Monterey pepper jack cheese, or more to taste

Salt and freshly ground pepper to taste

¼ cup chopped fresh parsley, for garnish (optional)

Set the bacon in the cooker and turn the heat to medium-high. Fry until quite crisp, stirring frequently to prevent sticking, and lowering the heat to medium, if needed, to prevent the bacon from burning, about 4 minutes. Transfer the bacon to a bowl and pour off all but a thin film of fat.

Add the onions and cook over medium-high heat, stirring frequently, until softened slightly, about 2 minutes. Add the coffee and stir well, taking care to scrape up any browned bits that are sticking to the bottom of the cooker.

Add the Worcestershire sauce, beef, and bay leaves. Stack the potatoes on top of the beef. (Some will end up in the liquid and become extremely soft and flavorful.)

Lock the lid in place. Over high heat, bring to high pressure. Reduce the heat just enough to maintain high pressure and cook for 20 minutes. Allow the pressure to come down naturally for 15 minutes. Quick-release any remaining pressure. Remove the lid, tilting it away from you to allow excess steam to escape.

With a slotted spoon, lift the potatoes out of the cooker and set them in a large bowl. Taste the beef and, if it is not sufficiently tender, return to high pressure for 5 minutes more. Again, let the pressure come down naturally.

Use a potato ricer or fork to mash the potatoes coarsely, mixing in the cheese and reserved, crisped bacon as you go. Season the potatoes with salt and lots of pepper. Reheat the potatoes in a microwave, if necessary.

Remove the bay leaves from the stew and season to taste. Ladle the stew into large, shallow bowls. Set a large mound of smashed potatoes in the middle. Garnish with parsley, if you wish.

SERVES 4

RUSSIAN PICKLED BEEF STEW

In Russian this soupy stew is called solianka, *a most lyrical name if ever I heard one. Solianka is likely to introduce you to a new world of taste combinations. That is, unless you've already had beef and potatoes combined with diced pickles, capers, and olives.*

For best results, use the real Jewish full-sour dill pickles. These will look more aged and olive green than the "new" or "half" sours. They may come whole or sliced into spears. Be sure you like the taste of the pickle you use since its flavor dominates the stew.

A dollop of Horseradish Cream adds a final kick to this most unusual dish, and fresh pumpernickel bread with sweet butter is the ideal accompaniment.

15 MINUTES HIGH PRESSURE PLUS 10-MINUTE NATURAL PRESSURE RELEASE

1 tablespoon sweet butter

2 cups thinly sliced leeks or coarsely chopped onions

4 cups beef or chicken broth

One 15-ounce can diced tomatoes, with liquid

2½ pounds boneless beef chuck, cut into ¾-inch pieces, well trimmed

½ cup diced smoked ham or pork butt

1 cup diced dill pickles

⅓ cup pitted, chopped Mediterranean olives, such as kalamatas

3 tablespoons drained capers

2 teaspoons dried dillweed

2 large bay leaves

2 pounds Yukon Gold potatoes, peeled and cut into 2-inch chunks

1 clove garlic, pushed through a press

Salt to taste

HORSERADISH CREAM

1 cup sour cream

2 to 4 tablespoons prepared horseradish, preferably white

Heat the butter in the cooker. When it begins to foam, add the leeks and cook over medium-high heat, stirring frequently, for 1 minute. Stir in the broth, tomatoes, beef, ham, pickles, olives, capers, dill, and bay leaves. Set the potatoes on top.

Lock the lid in place. Over high heat, bring to high pressure. Reduce the heat just enough to maintain high pressure and cook for 15 minutes. Allow the pressure to come down naturally for 10 minutes. Quick-release any remaining pressure. Remove the lid, tilting it away from you to allow excess steam to escape.

Remove the bay leaves. Stir in the garlic and salt (you may not need any), and simmer until the garlic loses its raw taste, about 3 minutes. During this time, slash the potatoes into bite-sized pieces, if you wish.

To prepare the Horseradish Cream: Blend the sour cream with 2 tablespoons of horseradish in a small bowl. Add more horseradish if you wish. (The amount you need will depend on your taste and on the strength of the horseradish.)

Serve each portion in a large bowl with a dollop of horseradish sour cream on top. Pass any remaining sour cream on the side.

SERVES 6

CUBAN MINCED BEEF WITH RAISINS AND GREEN OLIVES

Known as picadillo, *this zesty Cuban lunch-counter favorite combines beef with raisins, pimento-stuffed olives, and capers. Taking the lead from Joyce Lafray's recipe for Picadillo Magnifico in* Cuba Cocina!, *I've added diced potatoes, which complement the spices and transform the mixture into an easy one-pot meal.*

Because the beef is cut into such small pieces, the cooking time is considerably reduced. This quick, one-pot meal is likely to become one of your weekday supper favorites. Good on its own and nice over rice.

15 MINUTES HIGH PRESSURE

3 MINUTES ADDITIONAL COOKING

1 tablespoon olive oil

2 cups coarsely chopped onions

1 teaspoon whole cumin seeds

1 1/2 pounds boneless beef chuck, cut into 1/2-inch pieces, well trimmed

1/2 cup water

2 large bay leaves

1/4 to 1/2 teaspoon crushed red pepper flakes

Salt and freshly ground black pepper to taste

1 1/2 pounds Yukon Gold or red-skinned potatoes, scrubbed and cut into 2-inch chunks (peeling optional)

One 15-ounce can diced tomatoes with green chiles, with liquid, or Mexican-style tomatoes, coarsely chopped, plus 1 to 2 fresh jalapeños, seeded and chopped

1/3 cup dark raisins

2 large cloves garlic, pushed through a press

1 teaspoon dried oregano leaves

1/3 cup coarsely chopped pimento-stuffed olives

2 tablespoons drained capers

3 tablespoons chopped fresh cilantro, for garnish

Heat the oil in the cooker over medium-high heat. Cook the onions for 1 minute, stirring frequently. Add the cumin and cook for an additional minute. Stir in the beef and continue cooking, stirring frequently, until the beef loses its red color, 2 to 3 minutes. Add the water and stir well, taking care to scrape up any browned bits sticking to the bottom of the cooker.

Add the bay leaves, red pepper flakes, salt and pepper. Set the potatoes on top. Pour on the tomatoes with chiles (including canning liquid), but *do not stir*. Sprinkle the raisins on top.

Lock the lid in place. Over high heat, bring to high pressure. Lower the heat to maintain high pressure and cook for 15 minutes. Quick-release the pressure. Remove the lid, tilting it away from you to allow any excess steam to escape.

If the beef is not sufficiently tender, remove the potatoes and return to high pressure for 5 minutes more. Stir in the garlic, oregano, olives, and capers. Simmer over medium heat until the garlic loses its raw taste, 2 to 3 minutes. Meanwhile, slash the potatoes into bite-sized pieces—you can do this right in the cooker—and stir them in. Add salt and pepper, if needed. Garnish individual portions with cilantro.

SERVES 4

BEEF STEWED IN COCONUT MILK WITH RICE NOODLES AND GREEN BEANS

When cooked in coconut milk, beef takes on a rich and distinctly Asian flavor and tastes like it's been simmering all day. But this dish is actually remarkably quick and easy to prepare.

Once the beef is tender, you'll add very thin rice-stick noodles called "vermicelli." Rice vermicelli are available in Asian markets and look like a tangle of ivory-colored pasta. If you've purchased a 1-pound package, it can be a bit messy to pull apart the amount you need. Do it over the sink and don't be concerned if you have a little more or less than 4 ounces. These quick-cooking noodles are simmered in the stew after the pressure is released. They are long and slurpy, most easily eaten with chopsticks. If you can't find these noodles, angel hair pasta (capellini) makes a good substitute. Cook them separately according to package directions and add them just before serving.

If you have any leftovers, the noodles will continue to absorb liquid and the stew will become very thick. You can serve the dish as is or thin it with beef or chicken broth. An extra squeeze of lime juice will pick up the flavors.

15 MINUTES HIGH PRESSURE

3 TO 5 MINUTES ADDITIONAL COOKING

1 tablespoon peanut or canola oil

1 cup coarsely chopped onions

2 teaspoons whole cumin seeds

One 14-ounce can light, unsweetened coconut milk

1 tablespoon minced fresh ginger

1 teaspoon ground turmeric

1/2 teaspoon crushed red pepper flakes

1 teaspoon salt, or to taste

1 1/2 pounds boneless beef chuck, cut into 1/2-inch pieces, well trimmed

2 small cloves garlic, pushed through a press

4 ounces rice vermicelli, soaked in ample water to cover for 15 minutes, then drained

¾ pound string beans, trimmed and cut into 1-inch pieces, or one 10-ounce package frozen cut string beans (rinse away any ice crystals)

1 red bell pepper, seeded and finely diced

1 to 2 tablespoons freshly squeezed lime juice

Heat the oil in the cooker over medium-high heat. Cook the onions and cumin, stirring frequently, for 2 minutes. Add the coconut milk, ginger, turmeric, red pepper flakes, salt, and beef.

Lock the lid in place. Over high heat, bring to high pressure. Lower the heat to maintain high pressure and cook for 15 minutes. If time permits, let the pressure drop naturally. Otherwise, quick-release the pressure. Remove the lid, tilting it away from you to allow any excess steam to escape. If the beef is not sufficiently tender, return to high pressure for 5 minutes more.

Add the garlic. Stir in the noodles, taking care to submerge them in the liquid. Set the string beans and red pepper on top and set (but do not lock) the lid in place. Cook over medium heat at a gentle boil until the noodles are done and the beans are tender but still a bit crunchy, 3 to 5 minutes.

Stir in just enough lime juice and salt, if needed, to achieve a pleasing balance of flavors. Serve in large, deep bowls.

SERVES 3 TO 4

POT ROAST WITH POTATOES AND CARROTS

Fans of pot roast all agree that the roast should be cooked the night before and refrigerated overnight for optimum flavor. This approach also facilitates the removal of fat. (If you haven't planned ahead, you can degrease the broth using a gravy separator.) In either case, just before serving, cook the potatoes and carrots as directed below and then reheat the sliced beef in the broth.

Some people like to use rump or round for pot roast, but I find these cuts much too dry. Instead, look for a roast from any part of the chuck, which may be labeled eye, under-blade, top-blade (aka chicken steak), arm steak, or mock tender.

To produce a flavorful gravy, lightly brown the chopped vegetables at the start to bring out their sweetness, and puree them in the broth after cooking. This approach creates such a tasty gravy that it's not necessary to brown the roast.

1 HOUR HIGH PRESSURE PLUS 15-MINUTE NATURAL PRESSURE RELEASE (ROAST)

5 MINUTES HIGH PRESSURE (VEGETABLES)

1 tablespoon butter or vegetable oil

1 cup coarsely chopped onions

1/2 cup peeled and diced carrot

1/2 cup diced celery

3 to 3 1/2 pounds boneless beef chuck roast, well trimmed

4 small cloves garlic, peeled and cut into 1/2-inch-long slivers

Salt and freshly ground black pepper to taste

1/2 cup dry red wine or beef broth

1 1/2 cups beef broth

2 large bay leaves

1 teaspoon dried thyme leaves

2 teaspoons minced garlic

3 1/2 pounds Yukon Gold potatoes, peeled and cut into 1 1/2-inch chunks

1 pound carrots, peeled and cut into 2-inch chunks, or ready-to-eat baby carrots

1/4 cup chopped fresh parsley, for garnish

Heat the butter over medium-high heat until it begins to foam. Reduce the heat to low and add the onions, carrot, and celery. Cook, stirring every minute or so, until the vegetables have softened and the onions are lightly browned, about 5 minutes.

Meanwhile, with a paring knife, make shallow incisions all around the roast and press the garlic slivers into them with your finger. Season with salt and pepper. (Be sparing on the salt if you are using canned beef broth.)

When the onions are lightly browned, add the ½ cup of wine or broth. Stir well and be sure to scrape up any browned bits sticking to the bottom of the cooker. If using wine, cook over high heat until reduced by about half, 1 to 2 minutes. Add the 1½ cups beef broth and the bay leaves. Place the roast in the liquid, broad side down, arranging it so that the maximum surface possible is submerged in the liquid. (Don't be concerned if the roast touches the sides of the cooker; it will shrink as it cooks.)

Lock the lid in place. Over high heat, bring to high pressure. Reduce the heat just enough to maintain high pressure and cook for 1 hour. If you like your pot roast beyond fork tender and actually falling apart, increase the time under pressure to 1 hour and 15 minutes. Allow the pressure to come down naturally, about 15 minutes. Remove the lid, tilting it away from you to allow excess steam to escape.

Test the roast for doneness: You should be able to pierce it easily with a two-pronged fork and the meat should be very easy to chew. If the roast is not sufficiently tender, return it to high pressure for 10 minutes more. Again, allow the pressure to come down naturally.

Transfer the roast to a carving board and let it rest for 5 or 10 minutes before slicing. Remove the bay leaves. If not refrigerating overnight, strain and degrease the broth, using a gravy separator. Return the broth and chopped vegetables to the cooker. Stir in the thyme and minced garlic and add the potatoes and carrots.

Lock the lid in place. Over high heat, bring to high pressure. Reduce the heat just enough to maintain high pressure and cook for 5 minutes. Quick-release the pressure. Remove the lid, tilting it away from you to allow excess steam to escape. If the vegetables are not quite cooked, set (but do not lock) the lid in place and simmer over medium heat until done.

With a slotted spoon, transfer the potatoes and carrots to a warm platter and cover with foil. If you wish to thicken the gravy, puree the finely chopped vegetables (those that were cooked with the roast) and broth, adding a piece of potato or two if needed. Season with salt and pepper to taste. Slice the meat or, if easier, tear it into chunks. Reheat the meat in the gravy, if necessary. Arrange the meat, potatoes, and carrots attractively on a platter and spoon some gravy on top. Garnish with parsley. Pass the remaining gravy at the table.

SERVES 6

POT ROAST WITH POTATOES, TURNIPS, AND PEARL ONIONS

Substitute 1½ pounds peeled, purple-topped turnips, cut into 1-inch cubes, for 1½ pounds potatoes. Add 1 pint peeled pearl onions. Proceed as directed.

POT ROAST WITH FRUITED GRAVY

Just before adding the potatoes and carrots, stir 1½ cups chopped or snipped mixed dried fruit into the gravy. Proceed as directed. If your cooker has a thin bottom, set it on a Flame Tamer (page 4) to avoid scorching.

CORNED BEEF AND CABBAGE

If you love corned beef and cabbage, but never find the half-day required to let the brisket simmer, here's good news: The pressure cooker produces a fork-tender corned beef dinner in about 1½ hours.

For even cooking, avoid a chunky, thick piece of brisket and opt for a long, flatter one instead. It's fine to squeeze the brisket into the cooker, even if the meat is tightly pressed against the sides of the pot. Believe me, it won't be a squeeze for long: Corned beef shrinks about 50 percent as it cooks. It's a dense meat, and a few thin slices per person usually do nicely. However, if serious corned beef lovers are coming to dinner, this recipe may serve only 4.

For instructions on preparing potatoes and carrots instead of (or in addition to) cabbage, see below. It's fun to serve a variety of mustards with the corned beef, plus some Horseradish Cream—which goes especially well with cabbage and potatoes. If you have any leftovers, how about Reuben sandwiches for lunch?

70 MINUTES HIGH PRESSURE PLUS 15-MINUTE NATURAL PRESSURE RELEASE (CORNED BEEF)

4 MINUTES HIGH PRESSURE (CABBAGE)

3 pounds corned beef brisket
6 cups water, approximately
2 large bay leaves
1 large green cabbage (about 3 pounds), outer leaves discarded
Salt and freshly ground pepper to taste
Chopped fresh parsley, for garnish (optional)
Spicy brown mustard (plus other types) and/or Horseradish Cream (page 50)

Set the corned beef plus any juices accumulated in the blister pack in the cooker. Pour on water to cover by ½ inch. Submerge the bay leaves in the water.

Lock the lid in place. Over high heat, bring to high pressure. Reduce the heat just enough to maintain high pressure and cook for 70 minutes. Allow the pressure to come down naturally, about 15 minutes. Remove the lid, tilting it away from you to allow excess steam to escape.

If the corned beef is done, it should easily shred when pulled with a fork. If the beef requires more cooking, return it to high pressure for 5 minutes more and again allow the pressure to come down naturally. When the beef is tender, transfer it to a platter, lightly cover it with foil, and set it aside to cool. (Do not attempt to slice the beef when it is still quite hot as it will shred.)

Halve the cabbage and cut each half into 3 wedges, leaving the core intact to hold the leaves together. Submerge as many pieces of cabbage as you can in the broth. (If the broth reaches higher than three-quarters up the sides of the cooker, ladle some out.) Lock the lid in place. Over high heat, bring to high pressure. Reduce the heat just enough to maintain high pressure and cook for 4 minutes. Quick-release the pressure under cold running water.

If the cabbage is not sufficiently tender, gently stir it so that the wedges on top become submerged in the liquid. Then set (but do not lock) the lid in place and cook over medium heat at a gentle boil until the cabbage is done, 2 to 3 minutes more.

Carve the corned beef into thin slices across the grain, starting at one corner of the slab. With a slotted spoon, lift out the cabbage wedges, arrange them on a platter, and reserve in a warm place. If the corned beef needs reheating, place the slices in the broth and simmer until hot. Lift the slices out with a slotted spoon and arrange them on the platter. Season the cabbage with salt (if needed), pepper, and a bit of parsley, if you'd like to add some color. Serve with mustard and/or Horseradish Cream.

SERVES 4 TO 6

CORNED BEEF WITH CARROTS AND NEW POTATOES

Submerge 3 pounds of small (about 1½ inches diameter) white or red new potatoes (or larger potatoes, cut into 1½-inch chunks) in the corned beef broth. Add 6 carrots, peeled and cut into 2-inch chunks. If cooking cabbage along with carrots and potatoes, add only as much as will loosely fit 2 inches below the cooker's rim. Cook under high pressure for 5 minutes. If the vegetables are not sufficiently tender, set (but do not lock) the lid in place and cook over medium heat until done. Drain off the broth. Toss the vegetables in butter, if you wish, and lightly season with salt and pepper. Garnish with chopped parsley.

BEEF BRISKET WITH SAUERKRAUT AND POTATOES

For those who like their beef meltingly soft, brisket is a particularly pleasing cut to cook under pressure. Combined with sauerkraut and potatoes, this dish is bistro comfort food at its best.

If you can find it, use a well-trimmed second-cut brisket, which is more flavorful than the first-cut section. Because the second cut is fattier, be sure to refrigerate the dish overnight so that you can thoroughly remove the congealed fat. (If using a first cut, this won't be necessary.)

Whichever cut you use, you'll start out with what feels like a fairly substantial amount of meat, but keep in mind that the brisket will shrink about 25 percent. Sometimes it becomes so tender that you'll find it impossible to cut the meat into neat slices. In this case, just shred it into portion sizes.

Serve this dish with one or more varieties of mustard.

45 MINUTES HIGH PRESSURE PLUS 15-MINUTE NATURAL PRESSURE RELEASE (BRISKET)

5 MINUTES HIGH PRESSURE (POTATOES)

3 pounds fresh (refrigerated) sauerkraut

4 strips bacon, chopped

2½ to 3 pounds boneless beef brisket, well trimmed

1 tablespoon vegetable oil (optional)

1 cup coarsely chopped onions

1¾ cups beef or chicken broth, or more if needed

¾ teaspoon caraway seeds

3 pounds Yukon Gold or red-skinned potatoes, scrubbed or peeled and cut into 1½-inch chunks

Salt and freshly ground black pepper to taste

⅓ cup chopped fresh dill or parsley, for garnish

Drain the sauerkraut, reserving the brine for possible use in flavoring the final dish. Taste the kraut and, if it seems terribly salty, rinse it lightly or until it tastes just a bit stronger than you might like in the final dish. (The flavor will be diffused when the kraut is combined with the other ingredients.) Set aside.

Set the cooker over medium-high heat and cook half of the bacon, stirring frequently, until it renders a thin film of fat, 1 to 2 minutes. Add the brisket. (Cut it in half, if necessary, so that it will fit.) Brown the brisket well, lifting it up every minute or so to prevent sticking, about 3 minutes on each side. If necessary, add a tablespoon of oil to facilitate browning. Remove pieces of bacon if they begin to burn and set aside in a small bowl. Set the browned brisket aside.

Add the remaining chopped bacon and the onions and cook over medium-high heat, stirring frequently, until the onions are slightly softened, about 2 minutes. Add the broth (step back to avoid sputtering oil) and stir, taking care to scrape up any browned bits stuck to the bottom of the cooker.

Set the brisket in the broth and smother it with the sauerkraut. Lock the lid in place. Over high heat, bring to high pressure. Reduce the heat just enough to maintain high pressure and cook for 45 minutes. Allow the pressure to come down naturally for 15 minutes. Quick-release any remaining pressure. Remove the lid, tilting it away from you to allow excess steam to escape.

Remove the brisket and set it on a cutting board. After it has cooled for about 5 minutes, if it's still in one piece, slice it in half crosswise. Carve each half into thin slices across the grain or, if the brisket is too soft to carve, shred it into chunks. If the brisket is juicy and tender, set it aside. If the brisket is a bit tough or dry, submerge the slices (or pieces) in the sauerkraut in the cooker. If there is no liquid under the sauerkraut, add ½ cup broth or water.

Sprinkle the caraway seeds on the sauerkraut and pile the potatoes on top. Lock the lid in place. Over high heat, bring to high pressure. Reduce the heat just enough to maintain high pressure and cook for 5 minutes. Quick-release the pressure. Remove the lid, tilting it away from you to allow excess steam to escape.

If you've set the sliced brisket aside, transfer it to the pot to rewarm. Taste the broth and, if it needs more flavor, stir in the reserved sauerkraut brine plus salt and pepper to taste. Transfer to plates with a slotted spoon. Sprinkle the dill and any reserved crisp bacon bits on top.

Moisten the brisket with a bit of the gravy remaining in the cooker and pass any remaining gravy in a sauce boat.

SERVES 6

SHORT RIBS IN PASTA SAUCE WITH OLIVES AND PARMESAN POTATOES

Pasta sauce gives this stew an appealing burnt-orange hue, and it's a striking dish to serve company. Peeled potatoes are cooked on top of the beef, then removed and "smashed" with grated Parmesan, giving them an elegant finish. You can easily vary the taste of the stew by using a pasta sauce with sausage and peppers one time and mushrooms another.

Both short ribs and oxtails (see variation, page 65) are delicious cuts of beef that quickly cook to fork-tenderness in the pressure cooker. However, since these cuts contain hard-to-trim fat, it's ideal to refrigerate the cooked dish overnight so that you can remove the congealed fat from the surface.

Short ribs are usually sold in pieces about 2 inches thick and from 2 to 7 inches long. If only boneless ribs are available, you can use them; reduce the amount to 2 pounds. You may also substitute flanken, which are cut across the ribs in a different direction; cut the flanken between the ribs into portion sizes, if that hasn't been done already.

In any case, 35 minutes of cooking time works for a variety of shapes and sizes. In fact, you'll find that most of the meat will be falling off the bone when you open the cooker. You can either discard all of the bones and shred the meat into bite-sized pieces, or leave whatever meat is still on the bone in place.

35 MINUTES HIGH PRESSURE PLUS 10- TO 15-MINUTE NATURAL PRESSURE RELEASE

1 tablespoon olive oil

1 ½ cups thinly sliced leeks or coarsely chopped onions

1 cup dry white wine or vermouth

3 ½ pounds meaty beef short ribs or flanken, trimmed of surface fat

3 large carrots, peeled and cut into 2-inch chunks

1 cup oil-cured, pitted black olives

2 cups pasta sauce

¼ to ½ teaspoon crushed red pepper flakes (optional)

3 pounds Idaho or russet potatoes, scrubbed or peeled and cut into 2-inch chunks

Salt and freshly ground black pepper to taste

2 tablespoons olive oil or butter (optional)

¾ cup freshly grated Parmesan cheese, plus more for garnish

3 tablespoons chopped fresh basil or parsley

Heat the oil in the cooker. Cook the leeks over medium-high heat, stirring frequently, for 1 minute. Add the wine and stir well. Continue cooking until about 25 percent of it has evaporated, 1 to 2 minutes. Add the beef, carrots, and olives and pour the pasta sauce on top. Sprinkle on the red pepper flakes (if using). *Do not stir.* Pile the potatoes on top of the sauce.

Lock the lid in place. Over high heat, bring to high pressure. Reduce the heat just enough to maintain high pressure and cook for 35 minutes. Allow the pressure to come down naturally, 10 to 15 minutes. Remove the lid, tilting it away from you to allow excess steam to escape.

Transfer the potatoes from the cooker to a large serving platter or bowl. Pour the stew through a large strainer and degrease the sauce in a gravy separator. (Or refrigerate overnight and discard the congealed fat.) Discard any loose bones and shred the meat into bite-sized pieces.

Return the degreased sauce, meat, and potatoes to the pot and reheat. Season with salt and pepper. When ready to serve, remove the potatoes and smash them coarsely with a ricer, adding olive oil (if using) and sprinkling on Parmesan as you go. Season the potatoes with salt, if needed. Set a mound of potatoes in the center of a serving platter or individual plates and surround with the short ribs and sauce. Garnish with basil and an extra sprinkling of grated Parmesan.

SERVES 4

OXTAILS STEWED IN PASTA SAUCE

Omit the short ribs and substitute 3½ pounds meaty oxtails cut into approximately 2-inch lengths. Proceed as directed in the recipe, but increase cooking time to 50 minutes high pressure. If the oxtails are not sufficiently tender, return to high pressure for 5 or 10 minutes more.

ASIAN HOT POT WITH SHORT RIBS AND RICE NOODLES

This dish is the kind of slurpy beef-and-noodle hot pot you might see in Asian restaurants. With its distinctive combination of seasonings—soy sauce, ginger, brown sugar, garlic, and toasted sesame oil—and its bright, crisp vegetables in contrast to the dark beef and mushrooms, this hot pot leaves a lasting impression.

After only 35 minutes in the pressure cooker, the short ribs are fork tender and falling off the bone. Once you've tossed away most of the bones, it may look like too little meat to serve four, but keep in mind that the meat is rich and filling. (For some background on short ribs, see the preceding recipe; for a description of rice vermicelli, see page 242.)

Once the beef is cooked, you'll add broccoli florets and cooked rice vermicelli to the broth, so be sure to allow time to degrease it in a gravy separator (or better yet, refrigerate overnight and remove the fat that congeals on top). Serve this soupy stew in large bowls with chopsticks or forks and soup spoons.

If you can't locate rice vermicelli, cooked angel hair pasta makes a good substitute.

35 MINUTES HIGH PRESSURE PLUS 10-MINUTE NATURAL PRESSURE RELEASE

3 MINUTES ADDITIONAL COOKING

3 cups water

1 ounce (10 to 12 large) whole dried shiitake or Chinese black mushrooms

¼ cup tamari or other Japanese soy sauce, or more if needed

2 tablespoons tightly packed dark or light brown sugar

¼ to ½ teaspoon crushed red pepper flakes

3 pounds meaty beef short ribs or flanken, trimmed of surface fat

1 small bunch broccoli

1 large red bell pepper, seeded and diced

2 large cloves garlic, pushed through a press

1 tablespoon grated fresh ginger

2 scallions, trimmed and thinly sliced (keep white and green parts separate)

4 ounces rice vermicelli, cooked (page 242), drained, and then rinsed under cold water

½ teaspoon toasted sesame oil, plus more to taste

1½ tablespoons toasted sesame seeds (page 243), for garnish

Begin bringing the water to a boil in the cooker. If the shiitakes have stems, snap them off. (You may either reserve them for stock or grind them to a powder in a spice grinder and add them to the stew.) Add the shiitake caps, tamari, brown sugar, red pepper flakes, and ribs.

Lock the lid in place. Over high heat, bring to high pressure. Lower the heat to maintain high pressure and cook for 35 minutes. Let the pressure drop naturally for 10 minutes. Quick-release any remaining pressure. Remove the lid, tilting it away from you to allow any excess steam to escape. Let the stew cool slightly before proceeding.

Set a large strainer or colander over a large serving bowl and ladle or pour the stew into the strainer. Discard any "naked" bones. Shred whatever meat has fallen off the bones, discarding any gristle as you go. Leave any meat still clinging to the bones intact, if you wish; otherwise shred it as well. You may either cut the shiitake caps into bite-sized pieces or leave them whole.

Ladle the broth into a gravy separator and return the defatted broth to the cooker (or refrigerate the solids and broth separately overnight and remove the congealed fat before proceeding).

Cut the florets from the broccoli stalks, leaving only an inch or so of stem. Slice the florets so that the tops are about 1 inch across. Peel the stems and halve lengthwise, then cut into ½-inch slices. Rinse and drain.

Bring the defatted broth to a boil. Stir in the broccoli, red bell pepper, garlic, ginger, and sliced scallion whites. Cook, uncovered, over medium-high heat at a gentle boil, stirring occasionally, until the garlic loses its raw edge and the broccoli and red bell pepper are tender-crisp, about 3 minutes.

Stir in the beef and shiitakes, and cook until they are thoroughly heated. Add the cooked vermicelli, toasted sesame oil, and 1 or 2 more tablespoons of tamari, if needed. Ladle into large bowls and garnish with the scallion greens and toasted sesame seeds.

SERVES 4 TO 6

CHICKEN AND TURKEY

CHICKEN UNDER PRESSURE

Will it be light meat or dark? Chicken lovers usually position themselves into one of the two camps and are often unwilling to cross the dividing line. Yet, as everyone who has ever cooked a whole chicken knows, the light breast meat cooks more quickly than the dark thigh and leg.

My own preference is for chicken thighs, which are easily divided into portion sizes, look attractive, and come out moist every time. Leaving the bone intact adds flavor and gives the stew a more robust look that is appealing in a one-pot meal. However, to accommodate all tastes, I have made the choice of chicken parts as flexible as possible in the recipes. Unless otherwise stated, assume that the weight refers to bone-in chicken. If you prefer boneless breasts or thighs, purchase 25 percent less than the recipe calls for to account for the weight of the bone, and reduce cooking time as indicated in the chart below.

Here is a quick reference list for timings, plus some observations on chicken parts. If you wish to cook both light and dark meat together, choose the longer cooking time. The breast meat may be a bit dry, but people who favor breast don't seem to mind.

CHICKEN PART	TIME UNDER PRESSURE	COMMENTS
bone-in thighs	12 minutes	moist and flavorful, ideal size and shape for individual servings
boneless thighs	10 minutes	convenient when chopping into pieces after cooking; buy about 25% less to account for weight of bone
drumsticks	12 minutes	moist and tasty, but meat falls away from bone in an unattractive way
bone-in split breasts	10 minutes	mild flavor; may be dry
boneless thighs and breasts, cut into 1-inch pieces	4 minutes	convenient and practical when combined with other quick-cooking ingredients

Additional Pointers

Always skin chicken. When cooked under pressure, the skin shrivels up in an unattractive way and infuses the sauce with unnecessary fat.

Browning skinned chicken is a challenge. You need lots of oil and elbow grease to prevent the pieces from sticking to the pot and shredding. After much experimentation, I decided to eliminate this step. Since I've built a good deal of color and flavor into the sauces, you're not likely to miss the added taste dimension that browning offers.

Feel free to substitute frozen chicken parts for fresh. Timing under pressure remains the same, and there's no discernable difference in the texture of the cooked chicken.

I don't recommend cooking chicken wings under pressure. They are difficult to skin and the meat falls off the bone in no time. If you buy a whole chicken and cut it up yourself, freeze the wings and reserve them for another use, such as making broth.

Salmonella alert: Wash all chicken parts before using. Use very hot water to wash your hands, the knife, and cutting board immediately after handling chicken.

LEMONY CHICKEN SOUP WITH SPINACH

Here's a contemporary version of the classic Scottish chicken, leek, and barley soup called "cock-a-leekie." It's good for all that ails you on a cold winter's night. If you prefer to use onions, they make a fine substitute for leeks and create a slightly sweeter broth.

When you're in a hurry, serve the chicken on the bone, but the soup is more attractive if you chop the meat and discard the bones. Since today's chickens are mild in flavor, it's necessary to cook the chicken in part broth and part water to achieve a rich-tasting soup. To avoid exceeding the pressure cooker's maximum fill line, the chicken is cooked in water and a quart of broth is added at the end. If you're using salted broth, reduce added salt accordingly.

12 TO 15 MINUTES HIGH PRESSURE

2 TO 5 MINUTES ADDITIONAL COOKING

1 tablespoon butter or oil

3 1/2 cups thinly sliced leeks or coarsely chopped onions

4 cups water

3 pounds chicken parts, preferably thighs, skinned

3 large ribs celery, cut into 1-inch slices

4 large carrots, peeled and cut into 1-inch chunks

1/2 cup pearl barley, rinsed

2 large bay leaves

1/4 teaspoon dried thyme leaves

Salt to taste

4 cups chicken broth

1 1/2 pounds fresh spinach, trimmed, chopped, and thoroughly rinsed, or
   two 10-ounce packages frozen chopped spinach

1/4 cup minced fresh dill

4 to 5 tablespoons freshly squeezed lemon juice (from 2 juicy lemons)

Over medium-high heat, heat the butter in the cooker until it begins to foam. Cook the leeks, stirring frequently, until they soften, about 5 minutes. (If using onions, for a sweeter taste, cook them, covered, over low heat for an additional 5 minutes, stirring from time to time.) Add the water and bring to a boil as you prepare and add the chicken parts, celery, carrots, barley, bay leaves, thyme, and salt.

Lock the lid in place. Over high heat, bring to high pressure. Lower the heat to maintain high pressure and cook for 12 minutes. Quick-release the pressure by setting the cooker under cold, running water. Remove the lid, tilting it away from you to allow any excess steam to escape.

With a slotted spoon, transfer the chicken parts to a cutting board. Taste the barley, and if it is still hard (it should be chewy but tender), return to high pressure for 3 minutes more.

Spoon off any fat visible on the surface. Remove the bay leaves and discard. Stir in the chicken broth and salt to taste and bring to a boil. Add the spinach and boil the soup over medium heat until the spinach is tender, about 2 minutes for fresh and 5 minutes for frozen.

When the chicken is cool enough to handle, remove the meat from the bone and chop or shred it into bite-sized pieces. Return it to the cooker. When the chicken is good and hot, turn off the heat and stir in the dill, lemon juice, and salt to taste.

SERVES 6 TO 8

THAI-INSPIRED CHICKEN SOUP

Substitute one 14-ounce can unsweetened coconut milk for 2 cups of the water. Omit the thyme and cook the soup with the finely chopped bulbs of 2 stalks fresh lemongrass. You may add 4 to 6 ounces small, shelled shrimp at the end and boil over medium heat until they turn pink, 1 to 2 minutes. Substitute cilantro or basil for the dill and use lime juice instead of lemon. Season with Japanese soy sauce (tamari or shoyu) instead of salt.

Note: If you can't find fresh lemongrass, look for Thai Kitchen's lemongrass bottled in a light brine. Do not use dried lemongrass.

MOROCCAN CHICKEN WITH PRUNES AND COUSCOUS "STUFFING"

Who could resist the romance of a recipe created in the Tangier kitchen of writer Paul Bowles? The inspiration for this dish comes from a tantalizing collection of recipes called The Good Food: Soups, Stews & Pasta by Daniel Halpern and Julie Strand. Say the authors: "Its unique combination of flavors makes this North African stew an unforgettable eating experience." I agree!

In keeping with the one-pot theme of this book, I've suggested stirring the couscous into the fragrant cooking liquid and letting it steep for a few minutes right in the cooker. This technique results in couscous that has a moist, stuffing-like consistency. If you're a fan of fluffy couscous, prepare it separately according to package directions and ladle the stew on top. For an exotic Moroccan accompaniment, slice some oranges and drizzle them with rosewater and a sprinkle of ground cinnamon.

4 OR 12 MINUTES HIGH PRESSURE

4 TO 5 MINUTES FOR STEEPING COUSCOUS

2 tablespoons olive oil

1 pound (3 medium) red onions, peeled, halved, and thinly sliced

2 teaspoons whole cumin seeds

1 cup chicken broth

2 tablespoons minced fresh ginger

1 teaspoon ground turmeric

1 teaspoon ground cinnamon

1 teaspoon salt, or to taste

A few twists of freshly ground black pepper

3 pounds chicken parts, preferably thighs, skinned, or 2 1/2 pounds boneless, skinless chicken, cut into 1-inch pieces

1 generous cup pitted prunes

1/2 cup coarsely chopped lightly toasted almonds (page 239)

1 1/2 cups couscous

1/4 cup chopped fresh parsley or cilantro

Heat the oil in the cooker over medium-high heat. Cook the onions and cumin, stirring frequently, for 2 minutes. Stir in the broth, ginger, turmeric, cinnamon, salt, and pepper. Add the chicken and set the prunes on top.

Lock the lid in place. Over high heat, bring to high pressure. Lower the heat to maintain high pressure and cook for 4 minutes for boneless chicken pieces or 12 minutes for chicken parts. Quick-release the pressure. Remove the lid, tilting it away from you to allow any excess steam to escape.

Stir in the almonds and adjust for salt, keeping in mind that extra will be needed to flavor the couscous. Return the mixture to a boil over high heat. Stir in the couscous and parsley and turn off the heat. Set (but do not lock) the lid in place and let the mixture sit until the couscous is tender and most or all of the liquid has been absorbed, 4 to 5 minutes. Add more salt, if needed.

SERVES 4 TO 6

TIP
This dish doesn't freeze well, but refrigerated leftovers are delicious when reheated.

CHICKEN GUMBO

Here's my streamlined version of the traditional Louisiana gumbo. The okra—gumbo is the African name for this vegetable—becomes meltingly soft and thickens the stew while the andouille sausage gives it fire and smoke. If you can't locate this type of sausage, use the best smoked sausage you can find and make the gumbo chili-hot by seasoning with Tabasco sauce after cooking. There's plenty of sauce, so stir in Ready Rice (page 31) at the end, or serve the gumbo over rice.

4 OR 12 MINUTES HIGH PRESSURE

3 MINUTES ADDITIONAL COOKING

½ pound andouille or other smoked sausage, cut into ¼-inch slices

1 tablespoon olive oil (optional)

4 scallions, thinly sliced (keep white and green parts separate)

1 cup chicken broth

1 tablespoon Worcestershire sauce

1 teaspoon dried thyme leaves

2 large bay leaves

2 large ribs celery, cut into ½-inch slices

1 large green bell pepper, seeded and diced

¾ pound fresh okra, trimmed and cut into 1-inch chunks, or one 10-ounce package frozen sliced okra (rinse away any ice crystals; (see Tip)

3 pounds chicken thighs, skinned and well trimmed, or 2½ pounds boneless, skinless chicken, cut into 1-inch pieces

One 15-ounce can diced tomatoes, or stewed whole tomatoes, coarsely chopped, with liquid

1 to 2 cloves garlic, pushed through a press

1 to 2 tablespoons filé powder, cornmeal, or quick-cooking polenta (optional)

Salt and freshly ground black pepper to taste

¼ cup chopped fresh parsley

Tabasco sauce

Heat the cooker over medium-high heat, and brown the sausage well on both sides, 4 to 5 minutes. Add olive oil, if needed, to prevent sticking. Set the sausage aside. If there is more than a thin film of fat in the cooker, tip out the excess.

Over medium-high heat, cook the sliced scallion whites, stirring frequently, for about 1 minute. Add the broth and take care to scrape up any browned bits sticking to the bottom of the cooker. Add the Worcestershire, thyme, bay leaves, celery, green pepper, okra, chicken, and half of the browned sausage. Pour the tomatoes on top. *Do not stir.*

Lock the lid in place. Over high heat, bring to high pressure. Reduce the heat just enough to maintain high pressure and cook for 4 minutes for chopped boneless chicken or 12 minutes for whole thighs. Quick-release the pressure. Remove the lid, tilting it away from you to allow excess steam to escape.

Remove the bay leaves. Stir well as you add the reserved sausage and garlic. If the stew is too thin, sprinkle on the filé or other thickener while stirring. Bring to a boil, then lower the heat to medium and simmer until the stew has thickened a bit and the garlic has lost its raw edge, about 3 minutes. Add salt and pepper. Stir in the scallion greens and parsley just before serving. Pass the Tabasco sauce at the table.

SERVES 6

TIP

If you can find only whole frozen okra, allow it to thaw slightly and then cut into 1-inch chunks. If you're an okra lover and have bought a 16-ounce package, feel free to use all of it.

CHICKEN GUMBO WITH POULTRY SAUSAGE

Instead of andouille, use a sliced smoked turkey or chicken sausage. You'll probably need to use 1 to 2 tablespoons of oil for the browning stage.

CHICKEN CREOLE

Omit the okra. Instead of sausage, use ½ pound smoked country ham, cut into ½-inch cubes. Omit browning the ham and cook the scallion whites in olive oil.

CATHY'S GUMBO WITH CORN

My colleague, cookbook author Cathy Walthers, likes to add 1 cup fresh or frozen corn kernels for the last minute or two of cooking. Although not traditional, the corn adds great color and crunch.

QUICK CURRIED RICE WITH CHICKEN

This moist and colorful pilaf—enriched with coconut milk and dotted with bright green peas—provides a creative way to enjoy leftover cooked chicken.

First you steam the rice under pressure, then you toss in the diced chicken just before serving. If the rice on the bottom of the cooker develops a thin crust, stir these golden nuggets right into the pilaf for an extra bit of tasty crunch.

My preference is to use a mild curry powder, but you can use a hot blend or add some cayenne, if you wish. Mango chutney makes a nice accompaniment.

3 MINUTES HIGH PRESSURE PLUS 8-MINUTE NATURAL PRESSURE RELEASE

1 TO 2 MINUTES STEEPING

1 tablespoon peanut oil or butter

1 teaspoon whole cumin seeds

1 teaspoon fennel seeds

2 cups extra-long-grain white rice

1 1/2 cups chicken broth

One 14-ounce can unsweetened coconut milk

1 1/2 tablespoons mild curry powder, or more to taste

1 teaspoon salt

1/4 cup boiling water, if needed

4 cups diced, cooked chicken, warmed

1 1/2 cups frozen peas (rinse away any ice crystals)

Heat the oil in the cooker over medium-high heat. Add the cumin and fennel seeds and cook, stirring constantly, until they turn a shade darker and become fragrant, about 30 seconds. (Take care not to burn the spices.) Toss in the rice and coat it with the oil. Stir in the broth, coconut milk, curry, and salt.

Lock the lid in place. Over high heat, bring to high pressure. Reduce the heat just enough to maintain high pressure and cook for 3 minutes. Allow the pressure to come down naturally for 8 minutes. Quick-release any remaining pressure. Remove the lid, tilting it away from you to allow excess steam to escape.

Ajust for salt and add more curry powder, if needed. If the rice is not quite tender, stir in the boiling water as you add the chicken and peas. Set (but do not lock) the lid in place and steam an additional minute or two in the residual heat until the peas are tender-crisp and the rice is done. Stir well before serving.

SERVES 4

CURRIED RICE WITH LAMB

Substitute an equal amount of diced, cooked lamb for the chicken.

VEGETARIAN VERSION

Use vegetable instead of chicken broth and substitute 1 pound of diced, baked tofu (available in health-food stores and some supermarkets) for the chicken.

MEDITERRANEAN CHICKEN WITH LENTILS AND SWISS CHARD

If you have a longing to be in the South of France, head for the kitchen and prepare this unusual stew. It's full of the evocative flavors and colors of that delectable part of the world.

Since chicken and lentils are both done in about the same amount of time, they make natural companions in the cooker. For a special taste treat, substitute the delicate French green lentils du Puy for the common brown variety. (The French lentils may require a few minutes additional cooking after you've released the pressure.)

In this recipe, thinly sliced chard stems and most of the leaves are cooked with the lentils, giving the stew added flavor and body. The remaining leaves are stirred in at the end. They quickly wilt and offer bright spots of verdant color. If you use ruby chard, the dish is especially pretty.

When fresh basil is not in season, it's nice to finish off the dish by topping each portion with a heaping teaspoon of your favorite pesto.

12 MINUTES HIGH PRESSURE

4 TO 5 MINUTES ADDITIONAL COOKING

1 1/2 pounds Swiss chard

1 tablespoon olive oil

2 cups thinly sliced leeks or coarsely chopped onions

1/3 cup dry white wine or vermouth

4 cups chicken or vegetable broth (or a combination)

2 teaspoons fennel seeds

1 1/2 teaspoons dried oregano

1 1/2 teaspoons dried rosemary leaves (broken into bits)

2 cups lentils, picked over and rinsed

3 pounds chicken parts, preferably thighs, skinned and well trimmed

1 large clove garlic, pushed through a press, or more to taste

1/3 cup finely chopped, oil-packed sun-dried tomatoes

1/2 teaspoon orange zest, or more to taste

Salt and freshly ground black pepper to taste

⅓ cup chopped fresh basil

Holding the chard in a bunch, trim off and discard the bottom inch of the root end. Slice the stems as thinly as possible. Rinse well and set aside. Chop the leaves. (It is not necessary to strip the stem from the leaves.) Rinse well and set aside.

Heat the oil in the cooker over medium-high heat. Cook the leeks, stirring frequently, for 2 minutes. Add the wine and cook over high heat until most of it evaporates, 2 to 3 minutes. Add the broth, fennel seeds, oregano, rosemary, and lentils and stir well. Add the chicken, chard stems, and all but about 3 tightly packed cups of the leaves. (Don't be concerned if the cooker is very full; the chard will quickly wilt as the cooker comes up to pressure.)

Lock the lid in place. Over high heat, bring to high pressure. Lower the heat to maintain high pressure and cook for 12 minutes. Quick-release the pressure. Remove the lid, tilting it away from you to allow any excess steam to escape. Stir in the garlic, sun-dried tomatoes, orange zest, and salt and pepper.

If the mixture seems dry, add ½ cup water. Stir in the remaining chard leaves, pressing them beneath the lentils so that they quickly wilt. Set (but do not lock) the lid in place and cook over medium heat, stirring once or twice, until the lentils are done and the chard is tender but still bright green, 4 to 5 minutes. Stir in the basil and add more orange zest, if you like.

SERVES 6

VEGETARIAN VERSION

Omit the chicken and use vegetable broth. Cook for 10 minutes under pressure. Serve over pasta or rice.

SICILIAN CHICKEN WITH OLIVES AND ESCAROLE

If you love olives even half as much as I do, this gutsy dish is going to become a regular. Use either the large green Sicilian olives or a mixed batch of good-quality Mediterranean olives, including kalamatas and picholine or niçoise. The sweet hint of raisins brings good balance to the saltiness of the olives and anchovies. Indeed, you're not likely to need added salt. (By the way, the anchovies melt into the sauce so most people won't realize they're there.)

You can serve Sicilian Chicken on its own, but there's an abundance of flavor-packed sauce that screams out for a bed of pasta or polenta (page 32). If you plan to serve the mixture over a starch, consider using boneless chicken pieces, which make for easier eating.

4 OR 12 MINUTES HIGH PRESSURE

1 tablespoon olive oil

2 cups coarsely chopped onions

6 anchovy fillets (oil-packed)

½ cup dry white wine or vermouth

½ cup chicken broth or water

1 cup green Sicilian olives or mixed high-quality Mediterranean olives

¼ to ½ teaspoon crushed red pepper flakes

1½ pounds escarole, coarsely chopped, thoroughly rinsed, and drained

2 pounds chicken parts, skinned and well trimmed, or 1½ pounds boneless, skinless chicken cut into 1-inch pieces

3 cups good-quality pasta sauce

¼ cup dark raisins

½ cup chopped fresh parsley

Salt and freshly ground black pepper to taste (optional)

1 cup freshly grated Parmesan cheese, for garnish

Over medium-high heat, heat the oil in the cooker. Cook the onions and anchovies for 2 minutes, stirring frequently. Add the wine and continue cooking until most of it evaporates, taking care to scrape clean any browned bits stuck to the bottom of the cooker, 1 to 2 minutes.

Stir in the broth, olives, and red pepper flakes . Add the escarole and set the chicken on top. Pour the pasta sauce over all and add the raisins. *Do not stir.* (Don't be concerned that the cooker will be filled beyond the maximum recommended capacity; the greens will shrink dramatically as the cooker comes up to pressure.)

Lock the lid in place. Over high heat, bring to high pressure. (This may take about 5 minutes.) Reduce the heat just enough to maintain high pressure and cook for 4 minutes for boneless chicken pieces or 12 minutes for chicken parts. Quick-release the pressure by setting the cooker under cold running water. Remove the lid, tilting it away from you to allow excess steam to escape.

Stir well as you add the parsley. Add salt and pepper, if needed, and serve in large, deep plates on its own or over spaghetti or polenta. Pass a bowl of Parmesan at the table for sprinkling on top.

SERVES 4 ON ITS OWN OR 6 OVER PASTA OR POLENTA

VEGETARIAN VERSION

Omit the anchovies and chicken and use vegetable broth or water instead of chicken broth. Cook the remaining ingredients for 4 minutes under pressure. Serve over pasta or polenta.

WEST AFRICAN CHICKEN STEW WITH SPICY SWEET POTATO-PEANUT SAUCE

In this recipe, as the chicken cooks, most of the chopped sweet potatoes dissolve into a puree and combine with the ginger and curry to create a thick and flavorful sauce. The sweetness of the potatoes is rounded out nicely by the peanut butter stirred in at the end.

To control the spiciness, I've suggested a conservative amount of ginger and crushed red pepper. If you like your foods good and hot, double the amount of each. This dish is filling on its own but especially dandy when served on a mound of white or brown rice.

12 MINUTES HIGH PRESSURE

1 MINUTE ADDITIONAL COOKING

1 tablespoon peanut or other vegetable oil

8 scallions, thinly sliced (keep white and green parts separate)

3 tablespoons tomato paste

2 cups chicken or turkey broth

1 1/2 tablespoons mild curry powder

1 tablespoon minced fresh ginger, or more to taste

1/4 teaspoon crushed red pepper flakes, or more to taste

1 teaspoon salt, or to taste

A few twists of freshly ground black pepper

3 pounds chicken parts, skinned and well trimmed

1 large red bell pepper, seeded and diced

2 pounds sweet potatoes, peeled and cut into 1-inch chunks

6 tablespoons peanut butter, preferably nonhydrogenated and crunchy-style

1 1/2 cups frozen peas (rinse away any ice crystals)

1/4 cup chopped fresh cilantro, for garnish

1/3 cup chopped, roasted peanuts, for garnish (optional but adds nice extra crunch)

Over medium-high heat, heat the oil in the cooker. Add the sliced scallion bulbs and tomato paste and cook, stirring constantly, for 1 minute. Add the broth, curry, ginger, red pepper flakes, salt, and pepper. Add the chicken and red bell pepper. Pile the sweet potatoes on top.

Lock the lid in place. Over high heat, bring to high pressure. Reduce the heat just enough to maintain high pressure and cook for 12 minutes. Quick-release the pressure. Remove the lid, tilting it away from you to allow excess steam to escape.

Set the peanut butter in a small bowl or measuring cup. Push the solid ingredients in the cooker aside and ladle out about ½ cup of the broth. Blend this broth into the peanut butter, then stir the mixture into the stew. Stir well so that most of the sweet potatoes dissolve into a thick sauce. Add salt and pepper to taste.

Stir in the peas and cook over medium heat until tender, about 1 minute. Just before serving, garnish individual portions with cilantro, scallion greens, and chopped peanuts, if using.

SERVES 6

"BARBECUED" CHICKEN WITH BEANS AND CORN

This zesty down-home dish calls for cooking chicken in your favorite barbecue sauce, then tossing in some beans and corn. Be sure to use a sauce you love, preferably one whose first ingredient is tomato puree or paste rather than vinegar; otherwise, you'll end up with too much acid in the final dish. I've had good results using a supermarket brand called Bull's Eye in the Smoky Mountain Honey and Original Western versions.

Don't be alarmed to see a veritable sea of thin sauce when you open the cooker. Just allow a few minutes to thicken it up and round out the assertive barbecue sauce flavor by stirring in instant polenta or cornmeal. If you find the sauce too sweet, stir in a dollop of mustard to balance it off.

To infuse the chicken with maximum flavor, marinate it in the barbecue sauce overnight—but this is not necessary to produce a tasty dish. Substantial on its own, but the plentiful sauce is put to best advantage when ladled over rice.

11 MINUTES UNDER PRESSURE

4 TO 5 MINUTES ADDITIONAL COOKING

1 tablespoon olive oil

2 cups coarsely chopped onions

1 cup water

4 pounds chicken parts, skinned and well trimmed

¾ cup prepared barbecue sauce, or more to taste

3 cups cooked black beans, or one 1-pound 15-ounce can, drained and rinsed

3 tablespoons instant polenta or cornmeal

1 large red bell pepper, seeded and diced

1½ cups fresh or frozen corn (rinse away any ice crystals)

1 tablespoon mustard (optional)

Salt and freshly ground pepper to taste

Heat the oil in the cooker over medium-high heat. Cook the onions until slightly softened, stirring frequently, about 2 minutes. Stir in the water, taking care to scrape up any browned bits sticking to the bottom of the cooker. Add a few pieces of chicken and smear some barbecue sauce on top. Continue stacking chicken pieces and coating each batch with sauce. *Do not stir.*

Lock the lid in place. Over high heat, bring to high pressure. Reduce the heat just enough to maintain high pressure and cook for 11 minutes. Quick-release the pressure. Remove the lid, tilting it away from you to allow excess steam to escape.

Set the cooker over medium-high heat and bring the stew to a boil. Stir in the black beans, instant polenta, and red pepper and cook over medium heat at a gentle boil, stirring frequently, for 3 minutes. Add the corn and cook another minute or two to finish thickening the sauce. During this time adjust seasonings with mustard and/or a bit more barbecue sauce and some salt and pepper, if needed, to intensify or balance the flavors. Serve in large bowls or deep plates.

SERVES 6 TO 8

CHICKEN AND SPINACH IN CURRIED PASTA SAUCE

Here's the recipe to try when you have 15 minutes to get dinner on the table. Give an exotic lilt to a good-quality pasta sauce by seasoning it with mild Madras curry powder—I recommend the Merwanjee Poonjiajee & Sons brand available in many gourmet shops—but you can use a hot curry blend, if you prefer. Cook the chicken with frozen, chopped spinach which forsakes its individuality to enhance and thicken the sauce. The resulting dish doesn't taste quite like something you'd eat in an Indian restaurant, but it does taste very good.

For best results, use a thick pasta sauce—the type spread on pizza. Classico brand pasta sauce works well.

Serve over Ready Rice (page 31) or stir in 2 cups of frozen rice a minute or two before serving. If you don't want to bother with rice, you might like to try the potato variation on page 89.

4 OR 12 MINUTES HIGH PRESSURE

1/2 cup chicken broth or water

3 1/2 pounds chicken parts, preferably thighs, skinned and well trimmed, or 2 1/2 pounds boneless, skinless chicken, cut into 1-inch pieces

Two 10-ounce packages frozen spinach (rinse away any ice crystals)

1 1/2 cups pasta sauce

1 tablespoon mild curry powder, or more to taste

Salt to taste

Chopped fresh cilantro, for garnish (optional)

Place the broth and chicken in the cooker. Place the frozen blocks of spinach on top. Pour on the sauce and sprinkle on the curry powder. Gently stir the curry powder into the sauce. (*Do not stir* the chicken into the sauce; the goal is to prevent scorching the pasta sauce on the bottom while the cooker is coming up to pressure.)

Lock the lid in place. Over high heat, bring to high pressure. Reduce the heat just enough to maintain high pressure and cook for 4 minutes for boneless chicken pieces or 12 minutes for chicken parts. Quick-release the pressure. Remove the lid, tilting it away from you to allow excess steam to escape.

Stir well. Taste the sauce, and add more curry powder and salt, if needed. Garnish portions with chopped cilantro, if you wish.

SERVES 5 TO 6

CHICKEN, SPINACH, AND POTATOES IN CURRIED TOMATO SAUCE

For the 12-minute version, set 2 pounds of Yukon Gold potatoes, peeled and cut into 2-inch chunks, on top of the spinach. Increase pasta sauce to 2 cups and curry to 4 teaspoons. Continue as directed. After cooking, if you wish, slash the potatoes into smaller pieces and gently stir them into the sauce. For the 4-minute version, cut the raw potatoes into 1-inch dice.

TURKEY UNDER PRESSURE

With the ready availability of fresh parts in addition to ground and smoked turkey, we no longer need to wait until Thanksgiving to enjoy this tasty bird. Because it is so full of flavor, turkey imbues soups and stews with rich taste, and because the meat is so lean, there is rarely the nuisance of degreasing. Throw in the fact that it usually costs less per pound than chicken, and turkey comes out a real winner for one-pot meals.

I prefer the dense texture of drumsticks, but if they're not available, thighs (or a combination of drumsticks and thighs) do well. The meat of drumsticks is firm and moist, but you have to remove little tendons after they are cooked, making the chopping more time consuming. Thigh meat is somewhat stringy, but there's no question that thighs are much easier to chop. Like most things in life, it's a trade-off.

Here are some details about what works best in the pressure cooker and how to choose from what is available. As with chicken, to avoid bacterial cont-amination, always use very hot water to wash your hands and cooking equip-ment after you touch raw turkey.

- Turkey is bred very lean so it's less important to skin the parts than it is with chicken. I sometimes don't bother to skin drumsticks, but will often skin thighs since it's so easy to do.

- Turkey parts take 30 minutes to cook under pressure. You can either let the pressure come down naturally or use a quick-release method.

- If you'd like to use frozen parts without defrosting, increase the cooking time to 40 minutes.

- Opt for small drumsticks, preferably no more than 1½ pounds each, to assure that they will easily fit in the cooker. It is not necessary that all of the drumstick be submerged in liquid for the meat to cook prop-erly. If you can't fit the whole drumstick horizontally in the cooker, rest the bony end against the side of the pot.

- Because of their compact shape, it's never a problem to fit turkey thighs in the cooker. Like drumsticks, they take 30 minutes under pres-sure to cook.

- Wings have tasty meat but are more of a nuisance to deal with when it comes to chopping. If you are partial to them, feel free to substitute them for drumsticks, but use more since they have less meat in pro-portion to bone.

SPLIT PEA SOUP WITH SMOKED TURKEY

This one's fast and full of flavor! It's particularly convenient if you can find chopped smoked turkey wings or boneless smoked breast, which can easily be divided into portions. Otherwise, after cooking it's a simple matter to slice the smoked turkey from the bone, dice it, and stir it back into the soup. Look for smoked turkey at the deli counter or among the luncheon meats if you don't spot it in the poultry section.

The split peas melt down into a puree which gets thicker on standing. Serve as is or thin with water or broth. Smoked turkey can be quite salty so adjust seasonings at the end.

12 MINUTES HIGH PRESSURE

1 tablespoon vegetable oil

1 1/2 cups coarsely chopped onions

6 cups water

1 1/2 cups green split peas, picked over and rinsed

3 large carrots, peeled, halved lengthwise, and cut into 1/2 -inch slices

3 large ribs celery, diced

2 large bay leaves

1/4 teaspoon crushed red pepper flakes (optional)

1 1/4 to 1 1/2 pounds smoked turkey wing or drumstick, or 3/4 pound boneless smoked turkey breast, diced

Salt to taste

Freshly ground black pepper, for garnish

Heat the oil in the cooker over medium-high heat. Cook the onions, stirring frequently, until they soften slightly, about 2 minutes. Add the water, split peas, carrots, celery, bay leaves, red pepper flakes, if using, and smoked turkey.

Lock the lid in place. Over high heat, bring to high pressure. Reduce the heat just enough to maintain high pressure and cook for 12 minutes. Quick-release the pressure under cold running water. Remove the lid, tilting it away from you to allow excess steam to escape.

continued

Stir well and remove the bay leaves. If you used a whole wing or drumstick, remove it with a slotted spoon and, when cool enough to handle, chop the meat into bite-sized pieces and return to the pot. Discard the bones. If you wish to thicken the soup slightly, mash a few pieces of carrot against the sides of the cooker and stir them in.

Add salt, if needed. Serve in large soup bowls, garnished with a few twists of black pepper.

SERVES 4 TO 6

SPLIT PEA SOUP WITH SMOKED TURKEY AND KALE

After cooking, stir in 4 cups finely chopped, tightly packed kale leaves and stems (about ¾ pound). Cover and boil over medium heat, stirring occasionally, until the kale is tender, 5 to 7 minutes.

SPLIT PEA SOUP WITH TURKEY SAUSAGE AND KALE

Omit the smoked turkey. Cut 1 pound sweet or spicy turkey sausage into ½-inch slices, and brown in 2 or 3 batches in the oil. (Add a bit more oil if needed.) Stir in the onions and cook about 2 minutes, stirring frequently. Add 2 cups of water and stir well, taking care to scrape up any browned bits sticking to the bottom of the cooker. Add the remaining water and proceed as directed in the recipe, cooking the browned sausage along with the split peas. After cooking, stir in the kale as directed in the variation above.

SMOKED TURKEY RISOTTO WITH CORN AND ROASTED RED PEPPER

This unusual risotto, with its confetti-like dots of corn and red pepper, celebrates the fetching ingredients of Tex-Mex cooking. If you really like smoky flavors, opt for smoked cheddar at the end.

For more information on preparing risotto, see page 212.

4 MINUTES HIGH PRESSURE

3 TO 4 MINUTES ADDITIONAL COOKING

1 tablespoon olive oil

½ cup coarsely chopped onions

1½ teaspoons whole cumin seeds

2 teaspoons minced garlic

1½ cups arborio rice

4 cups turkey or chicken broth

1½ cups diced smoked turkey (from drumstick, breast, or wings)

½ cup pimento-stuffed olives, each olive sliced in thirds

1 cup frozen corn (rinse away any ice crystals)

1 large red bell pepper, roasted (page 241), seeded, and diced

1 jalapeño pepper, seeded and diced (optional)

2 cups (about 4 ounces) loosely packed, shredded, smoked or sharp cheddar

¼ cup chopped fresh cilantro

Salt and freshly ground black pepper to taste

Heat the oil in the cooker over medium-high heat. Cook the onions, cumin, and garlic, stirring frequently, for 1 minute. Stir in the rice and coat with the oil. Add the broth, smoked turkey, and olives.

Lock the lid in place. Over high heat, bring to high pressure. Lower the heat to maintain high pressure and cook for 4 minutes. Quick-release the pressure by setting the cooker under cold running water.

continued

Remove the lid, tilting it away from you to allow any excess steam to escape. Boil over medium-high heat, stirring constantly, until the rice is tender but still chewy and the risotto loses most of its soupiness and becomes somewhat creamy and thick, 3 to 4 minutes. Stir in the corn, red pepper, and jalapeño. Turn off the heat and stir in the cheddar until the cheese is melted. Stir in the cilantro and add salt and pepper.

SERVES 4

SMOKED HAM RISOTTO

Substitute diced smoked ham or pork butt for the turkey.

VEGETARIAN VERSION

Omit the smoked turkey and use vegetable broth. For optimum taste, use smoked cheddar cheese.

TURKEY CHILI

This recipe uses both turkey sausage and ground turkey to create a lower-fat but very flavor-packed quick chili. Use ground dark-meat turkey, if it's available, for the fullest flavor. Warning: Some turkey sausages are very spicy, so choose with care.

The chili is colorful and quite soupy—nice over Polenta Presto or Ready Rice. Or, if you're serving it on its own, you might like to thicken it with some quick-cooking polenta.

3 MINUTES HIGH PRESSURE

2 TO 3 MINUTES ADDITIONAL COOKING

1 tablespoon olive oil, or more if needed

1/2 pound smoked turkey sausage, cut into 1/4-inch slices

2 pounds ground turkey, preferably dark meat

2 cups coarsely chopped onions

2 teaspoons whole cumin seeds

1 cup turkey or chicken broth

1 1/2 tablespoons mild chili powder, or more to taste

1/2 teaspoon salt, or to taste

1/4 teaspoon ground cinnamon, or more to taste

2 large green and 2 large red bell peppers, seeded and diced

One 15-ounce can diced or stewed tomatoes, with liquid

1 to 2 cloves garlic, pushed through a press

2 tablespoons quick-cooking polenta or cornmeal, or more if needed (optional)

Cilantro-Lime Cream (page 43), chopped cilantro, or plain sour cream, for garnish

Heat the oil in the cooker over medium-high heat. Brown the sausage well on both sides, adding more oil if necessary to prevent sticking. Set aside. Add the ground turkey to the fat remaining in the cooker, and cook, stirring constantly, taking care to break up clumps, until it is no longer pink, 2 to 3 minutes. Stir in the onions and cumin and cook for an additional minute, stirring frequently.

continued

Add the broth and scrape up any browned bits sticking to the bottom of the cooker. Stir in the reserved sausage, chili powder, salt, cinnamon, and bell peppers. Pour the tomatoes on top. *Do not stir.*

Lock the lid in place. Over high heat, bring to high pressure. Reduce the heat just enough to maintain high pressure and cook for 3 minutes. Quick-release the pressure. Remove the lid, tilting it away from you to allow excess steam to escape.

Stir in the garlic and more chili powder and cinnamon, if needed. If the chili is too thin, sprinkle on polenta while stirring. Cook over medium heat, stirring frequently, until the mixture thickens and the garlic loses its raw taste, about 3 minutes. Add salt to taste.

Serve in large bowls with the garnish of your choice.

SERVES 4 ON ITS OWN OR 6 OVER RICE

TURKEY AND KIDNEY BEAN CHILI

Reduce the ground turkey to 1 pound and cook the chili with 1½ cups cooked or one 15-ounce can red kidney beans, drained and rinsed.

MEXICAN TURKEY VEGETABLE STEW

This flavor-packed soupy stew (shall we call it a "stoup"?) uses the zesty ingredients of the Mexican kitchen. First, turkey parts are cooked in water and tomatoes, infusing the liquid with deep flavor. Then, while you are cutting the cooked meat from the bone, the vegetables are cooked under pressure. Return the diced turkey to the pot along with some corn and final seasonings to create a hearty and unusual dish. Have a fresh lime on hand in case you need some acid to make the flavors pop at the end.

I prefer the dense texture of drumsticks for this dish, but thighs are fine (and easier to cut up!) if that's what's available. (For some details on your choice of turkey parts, see page 90.)

Accompany the stew with warm tortillas or corn chips, and pass a bottle of Tabasco sauce at the table. For a quick version using chicken that takes only 4 minutes under pressure, see below.

30 MINUTES HIGH PRESSURE (TURKEY)

4 MINUTES HIGH PRESSURE (VEGETABLES)

2 MINUTES ADDITIONAL COOKING

1 tablespoon olive oil

1½ cups coarsely chopped onions

1¼ teaspoons whole cumin seeds

1 cup water

One 15-ounce can diced tomatoes with green chiles, with liquid, or stewed Mexican-style tomatoes, coarsely chopped

½ teaspoon salt, or to taste

3 pounds turkey drumsticks and/or thighs, skinned

1 pound Yukon Gold potatoes, peeled and cut into 1-inch chunks

2 large ribs celery, halved lengthwise and cut into ½-inch slices

2 large carrots, peeled and cut into 1-inch slices

1 large green bell pepper, seeded and diced

1½ cups fresh or frozen corn (rinse away any ice crystals)

1 to 2 cloves garlic, pushed through a press

1 teaspoon dried oregano leaves

¼ cup chopped fresh cilantro

1 tablespoon freshly squeezed lime juice, or more to taste (optional)

continued

Heat the oil in the cooker over medium-high heat. Cook the onions, stirring frequently, for 2 minutes. Stir in the cumin and cook for an additional 30 seconds or so. Add the water and take care to scrape up any browned bits sticking to the bottom of the cooker. Add the tomatoes and salt.

Set the turkey in the cooker fleshy side down. (Although the meat may not be entirely covered with liquid, it will cook properly.)

Lock the lid in place. Over high heat, bring to high pressure. Lower the heat to maintain high pressure and cook for 30 minutes. Quick-release the pressure by setting the cooker under cold running water. Remove the lid, tilting it away from you to allow excess steam to escape. With a slotted spoon, transfer the turkey to a cutting board.

Add the potatoes, celery, carrots, and green pepper to the broth in the cooker. Lock the lid in place. Over high heat, bring to high pressure. Reduce the heat just enough to maintain high pressure and cook for 4 minutes.

While the vegetables are cooking, carve the turkey meat from the bone and cut it into bite-sized chunks. When the timer for the vegetables goes off, quick-release the pressure. Remove the lid, tilting it away from you to allow any excess steam to escape. Stir in the corn, garlic, oregano, and chopped turkey. Simmer until the corn is cooked and the garlic loses its raw taste, about 2 minutes. Stir in the cilantro and perk up the flavors with lime juice, if needed. Serve in large soup bowls.

SERVES 4 TO 6

VARIATION

Substitute ¾ cup frozen peas or cooked black beans for half of the corn.

MEXICAN CHICKEN AND VEGETABLE STEW

Instead of turkey, use 2½ pounds boneless, skinless chicken parts, cut into 1-inch pieces. Substitute chicken broth for the water. Cook the chicken along with the potatoes, celery, carrots, and pepper for 4 minutes under high pressure. Proceed as directed above.

PORK AND SAUSAGE

PORK UNDER PRESSURE

Marketed in recent years as "the other white meat," pork nowadays has 57 percent less fat and 22 percent more protein than the pork of two decades ago, according to Merle Ellis, author of *The Great American Meat Book*. So if your butcher tries to talk you out of buying cubed pork shoulder or a boneless picnic shoulder roast in favor of a leaner cut, tell him that you don't want to go quite that lean. Why end up with dry, flavorless meat?

When shopping for fresh pork, look for moist pink meat with reddish bones and white fat. Avoid any pork with grayish bones and yellowing fat. Refrigerate for up to 3 days or until the expiration date on the package, whichever comes first.

Most of the recipes call for cubed pork shoulder, a moist and flavorful cut that is also (most confusingly) known as Boston butt, Boston shoulder, or Western butt. Packages labeled "stew meat" are likely to contain cubed shoulder or butt. If cubed pork is not available, you can buy a whole butt with or without the bone and cut it up yourself, freezing any extra for later use.

I don't, however, recommend buying a bone-in picnic shoulder to cube for stews. Although the meat is delicious and seems inexpensive by the pound, cutting it from the bone is a messy job and the bone, rind, and fat account for half of the weight, so it ends up being uneconomical. A boneless rib-end pork roast would be a better choice, if that's available.

Pork loin can cook up slightly dry (like chicken breast) but is a good alternative for those who prefer mildly flavored meat. When quarterloin or sirloin pork chops are on sale, they are an economical choice; just cut the meat into cubes. Buy about 30 percent more to account for the weight of the bones, and include any bones in the stew for added flavor. Discard them after cooking.

Avoid using pork leg as it's very lean and is likely to be quite dry and lacking in flavor. Look for details on other cuts in the headnotes to the recipes.

SAUSAGES

It takes very little of a high-quality sausage to add marvelous flavor to soups and stews. Unfortunately, the mass-fabricated sausages sold in most supermarkets pale in comparison to traditionally made varieties. It's worth going out of your way for the best. If your local butcher or gourmet shop doesn't sell good sausages, consider ordering a batch by mail (see page 245).

I've called for specific sausages to match the origin of each recipe (Portuguese linguiça in a Portuguese bean dish, and so on), but there's no reason why you can't substitute your own favorite type. Those who prefer low-fat turkey and chicken sausages may also use those.

If you wish to reduce the fat in any fresh (refrigerated) sausages, bring a quart of water to a boil in the cooker. With a fork, puncture the sausages about 10 times and boil them whole for 5 minutes. Drain and, when cool enough to handle, cut into ½-inch slices.

You'll find descriptions of specific sausages listed by type in the Guide to Ingredients, page 233.

CABBAGE AND POTATO SOUP WITH SWEET ITALIAN SAUSAGE

This simple dish comes from the tradition of Italian cucina povera (the food of the poor) which relies on a few humble ingredients masterfully combined to make the whole much greater than the sum of its parts.

Sausage infuses this soup with rich flavor, and tomato paste gives it an appealing pale orange hue. I prefer using sweet fennel sausage, but you can substitute the spicy variety, if you like. Add Savoy cabbage, potatoes, and a generous portion of Pecorino Romano, and you have a deeply satisfying one-pot meal. For more substance still, ladle the soup over thick slices of peasant bread.

3 MINUTES HIGH PRESSURE

1 pound fresh Italian pork sausages, cut into ½-inch slices
2 cups coarsely chopped onions
2 tablespoons tomato paste
8 cups chicken or turkey broth
2 pounds Idaho (russet) potatoes, peeled and cut into 1-inch cubes
1½ pounds Savoy cabbage, cored and shredded
¼ cup minced fresh parsley
1 cup freshly grated Pecorino Romano cheese
Salt to taste
6 slices hearty peasant bread (optional)
Freshly ground pepper to taste

Place the sliced sausage in the cooker and turn the heat to medium-high. When the sausage begins to sizzle, turn the heat to medium, stir, and continue to cook, stirring frequently, until the sausage is lightly browned, 2 to 3 minutes. Add the onions and tomato paste and cook, stirring frequently, 2 minutes more.

Add a few cups of broth and stir well to scrape up any browned bits stuck to the bottom of the cooker. Add the remaining broth, potatoes, and cabbage. (Don't be concerned if the contents exceed the maximum recommended capacity; the cabbage will wilt as you bring up the pressure.)

Lock the lid in place. Over high heat, bring to high pressure. (This may take longer than usual since the pot is so full.) Reduce the heat just enough to maintain high pressure and cook for 3 minutes. Quick-release the pressure by setting the cooker under cold running water. Remove the lid, tilting it away from you to allow excess steam to escape.

Stir in the parsley, ⅓ cup of Pecorino Romano, and add salt. If using bread, set a slice on the bottom of each bowl and ladle the soup on top. Sprinkle on a liberal portion of Pecorino Romano and black pepper. Pass any remaining cheese at the table.

SERVES 6

VARIATIONS

Substitute chopped chicory or escarole for the cabbage.

Use Italian-style chicken or turkey sausage instead of pork sausage.

BLACK BEAN SOUP WITH CHORIZO SAUSAGE

Here's a robust soup made from scratch in under half an hour—you don't even have to presoak the beans. The Spanish sausage called chorizo gives the soup both smokiness and heat. Feel free to substitute another smoked sausage if chorizo is not available.

This inky-black soup has so much flavor that it really needs no garnish. But if you'd enjoy a pop of bright color, scatter some diced tomato or avocado on top of each portion—and a sprinkling of chopped cilantro, if you're fond of it.

I like to use part broth and part water for a very rich rendition. If you follow suit, be sure your broth is unsalted; the smoked ham hock and chorizo usually provide enough salt for the entire soup.

Leftovers thicken into a stew. Ladle them over rice for your next meal, or thin them with broth or water.

22 MINUTES HIGH PRESSURE

5 MINUTES ADDITIONAL COOKING

1 tablespoon annatto oil (page 233) or plain olive oil

3 cups coarsely chopped onions

1 tablespoon minced garlic

2 teaspoons whole cumin seeds

1 tablespoon dried oregano leaves

1 tablespoon sweet paprika

4 cups water

4 cups unsalted chicken or turkey broth or additional water

2 1/2 cups (1 pound) black beans, picked over and rinsed

1 meaty smoked ham hock or turkey drumstick

1/2 pound chorizo or kielbasa sausages, halved lengthwise, then cut into 1/2-inch slices

2 large green bell peppers, seeded and diced

3 large bay leaves

2 tablespoons dry sherry

1/4 to 1/2 teaspoon crushed red pepper flakes (optional)

Salt to taste

Chopped cilantro, for garnish (optional)

Diced tomato or avocado, for garnish (optional)

Over medium-high heat, heat the oil in the cooker. Add the onions and cook, stirring frequently, for 2 minutes. Add the garlic, cumin, and oregano, and cook until the onions are soft, about 2 minutes more. Turn off the heat and stir in the paprika. Transfer the onion mixture to a small bowl and set aside.

Add the water and broth and turn the heat to high. Stir well to scrape up any browned bits stuck to the bottom of the cooker. Add the beans, ham hock, sausage, peppers, and bay leaves. Lock the lid in place. Over high heat, bring to high pressure. Reduce the heat just enough to maintain high pressure and cook for 22 minutes. Quick-release the pressure by placing the cooker under cold running water. Remove the lid, tilting it away from you to allow excess steam to escape. If the beans are not tender, return the soup to high pressure for 5 minutes more.

When the beans are tender, remove the bay leaves and ham hock. Stir in the onion mixture and sherry. If the soup isn't spicy enough, add some crushed red pepper flakes. Add salt, if needed. Boil uncovered over medium heat, stirring occasionally, for 5 minutes. Meanwhile, chop the meat from the ham hock (there won't be much) and add it to the soup. If you plan to serve the soup immediately and would like it thicker, mash about a cupful of the beans against the side of the cooker and vigorously blend the mash into the soup. Otherwise, leave the soup on the stove with the lid ajar for 30 minutes and it will thicken on its own. Garnish individual portions with cilantro and diced tomato or avocado, if you wish.

SERVES 7 TO 8

PORK WITH SAUERKRAUT, MUSHROOMS, AND POTATOES

This hearty cold-weather dish takes its inspiration from the kitchens of Eastern Europe. Dried mushrooms and sauerkraut infuse the stew with an earthy, robust flavor nicely balanced by potatoes and a hint of sour cream.

Most sauerkraut nowadays doesn't have the complex tang of traditional barrel-pickled cabbage. Rinsing, therefore, must be done with caution, or not at all. As an insurance policy, reserve the brine when you drain the kraut, so you can stir it in at the end to enhance the final flavor of the dish.

10 MINUTES HIGH PRESSURE

3 pounds fresh (refrigerated) sauerkraut

2 cups chicken or beef broth

1 ounce (1 cup loosely packed) dried mushrooms

1 tablespoon butter

1 tablespoon vegetable oil, or more if needed

3 pounds pork shoulder (butt) or loin, cut into 1-inch cubes, well trimmed

1 teaspoon caraway seeds

2 pounds Yukon Gold potatoes, peeled and cut into 2-inch chunks

¾ pound parsnips, scrubbed and cut into 2-inch chunks (or use 2 additional potatoes)

½ cup sour cream, plus more to pass at the table

Salt and freshly ground black pepper to taste

¼ cup chopped fresh dill, for garnish

Drain the sauerkraut and reserve the brine. Taste the sauerkraut and, if you find it much too strong, rinse it until you like the way it tastes—keeping in mind that the flavor will be diminished when it is cooked with the other ingredients. Drain well and set aside.

Heat the broth in the cooker. Set the dried mushrooms in a bowl and pour the hot broth over, submerging them in the broth with the back of a spoon. Cover with a plate and set aside until the mushrooms are soft, about 10 minutes.

Meanwhile, rinse and dry out the cooker. Heat the butter and oil over medium-high heat. Brown the pork in 3 or 4 batches, about 4 minutes per batch, adding more oil if needed. Set aside.

With a slotted spoon, remove the reconstituted mushrooms from the broth and squeeze them over the bowl to catch the liquid they release. Coarsely chop the mushrooms if the pieces are large. Carefully pour the broth into the cooker, taking care to leave behind any sediment on the bottom. Set the cooker over medium heat and stir well to scrape up any browned bits stuck to the bottom. Add the mushrooms and half of the sauerkraut. Set the browned pork on top. Cover with the remaining sauerkraut and sprinkle the caraway seeds on top. Set the potatoes and parsnips on the kraut.

Lock the lid in place. Over high heat, bring to high pressure. Reduce the heat just enough to maintain high pressure and cook for 10 minutes. Quick-release the pressure. Remove the lid, tilting it away from you to allow excess steam to escape.

Ladle out ½ cup of the broth and blend the sour cream into it. Then stir this mixture back into the pot as you stir well to distribute all of the ingredients. If you'd like a stronger sauerkraut flavor, add some or all of the reserved brine. Season with salt and pepper. Sprinkle lightly with dill. Pass additional sour cream in a bowl at the table.

SERVES 6 TO 8

PORK WITH KIELBASA AND SAUERKRAUT

Substitute an equal amount of sliced kielbasa for ½ to 1 pound of the pork shoulder. Browning the kielbasa is optional.

SWEET AND SOUR RIBS WITH PINEAPPLE

This recipe is an homage to the sixties and to the many vintage pressure-cooker recipes for this American favorite. Since I consider pressure cooking a great way to keep the flavors of home cooking alive, it's rather ironic that this dish happily tastes like something you'd get in a good Cantonese restaurant—pineapple and all.

Delicious as they are, spareribs can be cantankerous and tough. Most will cook to fork-tenderness in 25 minutes, but some batches may take as long as 30. If you can find them, opt for country-style ribs, which have a higher percentage of meat in relation to bone. Avoid packages labeled "spareribs," as they have the sternum bone still attached, making it difficult to cut the ribs into portion sizes; instead, choose barbecue ribs, which are sold without the sternum bone. If you prefer the smaller baby back ribs, reduce cooking time to 20 minutes under pressure.

Since the ribs look more attractive when they're browned, I recommend popping them under the broiler or on the grill while you're degreasing the sauce—but this is an optional step.

Serve the ribs and tasty sauce over Ready Rice (page 31) or stir 2 cups of Ready Rice into the sauce just before serving.

25 TO 30 MINUTES HIGH PRESSURE

ABOUT 5 MINUTES ADDITIONAL COOKING

⅓ cup water

2 cups thinly sliced onions

5 pounds meaty pork spareribs, preferably country-style

½ cup dry sherry

3 tablespoons apple cider vinegar

2 tablespoons tamari or other Japanese soy sauce, or more if needed

1 tablespoon brown or white sugar

¼ to ½ teaspoon crushed red pepper flakes (optional)

One 20-ounce can pineapple chunks in unsweetened pineapple juice

1 large red and 1 large green bell pepper, seeded and cut into 1/2-inch strips

1 tablespoon minced fresh ginger

1 to 2 cloves garlic, pushed through a press

2 tablespoons cornstarch blended into 2 tablespoons water, or more if needed

Place the water and sliced onions on the bottom of the cooker. Cut each rack of spareribs into serving sizes of 2 ribs each and trim off the surface fat. Stack the ribs on the bed of onions.

In a small bowl, combine the sherry, vinegar, tamari, sugar, and red pepper flakes, if using. Pour this mixture over the ribs. *Do not stir.*

Lock the lid in place. Over high heat, bring to high pressure. (This may take as long as 15 minutes because the cooker is so full.) Reduce the heat just enough to maintain high pressure and cook for 25 minutes. Quick-release the pressure. Remove the lid, tilting it away from you to allow excess steam to escape.

Check the ribs for doneness in several places by seeing if the meat can easily be pried away from the bone and by sampling a few bits. If the meat is not sufficiently tender, return to high pressure in 5-minute increments until done.

If you wish, set the ribs on a broiling pan, fleshy side up, and broil until nicely browned, 3 to 5 minutes. Otherwise, transfer the ribs from the cooker to a large bowl and cover loosely with foil. (Discard any "naked" bones as you go.) Degrease the sauce in a gravy separator and return it to the cooker. Add the pineapple chunks, with liquid, peppers, ginger, and garlic and cook over medium heat at a gentle boil, covered, for 3 minutes.

Stir in the cornstarch solution and continue to cook over medium heat, uncovered, stirring frequently, until the sauce thickens and the peppers are tender-crisp, about 2 minutes more. If the sauce doesn't become sufficiently thick, blend an additional tablespoon of cornstarch into a tablespoon of water, stir in, and continue cooking another minute or two. Add tamari, if needed, to give the sauce a good balance of sweet and salty. Pour the sauce over the ribs and serve.

SERVES 4

CARIBBEAN PORK STEW

This delightful stew calls for calabaza pumpkin and the starchy banana look-alike called plantain. Both are at the heart of the Caribbean diet, and are now available in many supermarkets. You will see the plantain at various stages of ripeness. When it's green, it's quite bland and starchy. Left at room temperature for 3 to 5 days to ripen and turn yellow, it becomes sweeter and less starchy. Eventually the plantain becomes quite blackened and sweet. This recipe calls for yellow plantains, but if there are a few black spots, that's fine.

The selection and handling of calabaza and plantain are described in the Guide to Ingredients (page 233), but if they are not available locally or you're not feeling adventurous, just substitute fresh or frozen squash for the pumpkin and Yukon Gold potatoes for the plantain. You'll still be rewarded with a delicious stew.

Be forewarned: The calabaza dissolves into a puree that thickens the stew and gives it a gorgeous orange color. The plantain retains its shape. Serve the stew on its own or over rice.

10 MINUTES HIGH PRESSURE

1 MINUTE ADDITIONAL COOKING

2 tablespoons annatto oil (page 233) or plain olive oil

2 cups coarsely chopped onions

2 pounds pork shoulder (butt) or loin, cut into 1-inch pieces, well trimmed

1 cup chicken or vegetable broth

1 teaspoon salt, or to taste

1/4 teaspoon crushed red pepper flakes, or more to taste

1 1/2 pounds calabaza pumpkin or butternut squash, peeled and cut into
    1-inch chunks, or two 12-ounce packages frozen squash (see Tip)

3 yellow or slightly blackened plantains, peeled and cut into 1-inch slices,
    or 1 1/2 pounds Yukon Gold potatoes, peeled and cut into 1-inch chunks

1 large red and 1 large green bell pepper, seeded and diced

One 15-ounce can diced tomatoes with green chiles, with liquid, or one
    15-ounce can diced tomatoes and 1 to 2 fresh jalapeños, seeded and diced

2 cups fresh or frozen corn kernels (rinse away any ice crystals)

1/4 cup chopped fresh cilantro

Tabasco or Caribbean hot sauce to taste

Heat the oil in the cooker over medium-high heat. Add the onions and cook, stirring frequently, until they have softened slightly, about 3 minutes. Add the pork and continue cooking and stirring until it loses its pink color, 3 to 5 minutes more.

Add the broth, taking care to scrape up any browned bits sticking to the bottom of the cooker. Add the salt, red pepper flakes, calabaza, plantains, and bell peppers. Pour the diced tomatoes on top. (If using fresh jalapeños, add them at the end.) *Do not stir.*

Lock the lid in place. Over high heat, bring to high pressure. Reduce the heat just enough to maintain high pressure and cook for 10 minutes. Quick-release the pressure. Remove the lid, tilting it away from you to allow excess steam to escape.

Stir in the corn and cilantro, plus additional salt, red pepper flakes, and Tabasco sauce to taste. Cook just until the corn is tender, about 1 minute. Serve in large, shallow bowls on its own or over rice.

SERVES 6

TIP
Don't hesitate to use frozen squash. It works very well in this context and saves you the trouble of peeling and chopping. Look for packages labeled "cooked squash," but avoid "fully prepared" frozen squash, which contains additional ingredients.

"BARBECUED" PORK WITH SWEET POTATOES

In this dish, a quickly made barbecue sauce infuses the pork with irresistible flavor, especially delicious when given the chance to marinate overnight. The sauce is slightly sweet, with a bit of mustard and chili sauce tang.

The sliced sweet potatoes that cook submerged in the liquid soften enough to dissolve and thicken the sauce. The chunked sweet potatoes stacked on top usually hold their shape well enough to be cut into bite-sized pieces. These are stirred into the stew at the end, offering nice bright spots of orange against the reddish brown sauce. This stew is a bit soupy, so serve it in large bowls, over rice if you wish.

10 MINUTES HIGH PRESSURE

¾ cup bottled chili sauce, such as Heinz

2 tablespoons spicy brown mustard or Dijon

2 tablespoons Worcestershire sauce

1 tablespoon maple syrup or brown sugar

2 pounds pork shoulder (butt) or loin, cut into ¾-inch pieces and well trimmed

1 tablespoon olive oil

2 cups coarsely chopped onions

2 large green bell peppers, seeded and diced

½ cup water

2½ pounds sweet potatoes, peeled and cut into 2-inch chunks

Salt and freshly ground black pepper to taste

In a large bowl, blend the chili sauce, mustard, Worcestershire, and maple syrup. Add the pork and toss to coat. Set aside for a few moments at room temperature or marinate, covered, in the refrigerator overnight or up to 16 hours.

Heat the oil in the cooker over medium-high heat. Cook the onions, stirring frequently, for 2 minutes. Add the green peppers and cook for another minute. Stir in the water, taking care to scrape up any browned bits sticking to the bottom of the cooker. Cut 4 pieces of sweet potato into thin slices and add them to the broth. Transfer the sauce-coated pork plus any unabsorbed marinade to the cooker. *Do not stir.* Set the remaining sweet potatoes on top.

Lock the lid in place. Over high heat, bring to high pressure. Reduce the heat just enough to maintain high pressure and cook for 10 minutes. Use a quick-release method. Remove the lid, tilting it away from you to allow excess steam to escape.

If the pork is not sufficiently tender, remove the large chunks of sweet potatoes, and return to high pressure for 5 minutes more.

If you wish, cut the sweet potatoes into smaller chunks. Stir the stew well. Add salt and pepper. Serve in large shallow bowls.

SERVES 4

TAMED PORK VINDALOO WITH SPINACH AND POTATOES

It's rare that I come across pressure-cooker recipes when browsing through cookbooks, but that's exactly what happened when I perused Madhur Jaffrey's Quick & Easy Indian Cooking. "A truly wonderful gadget," says Jaffrey of the pressure cooker, voicing the enthusiasm of most Indian cooks.

Here's Jaffrey's delightful recipe—truly quick and easy—which I've given one-pot status by adding spinach and potatoes. I've also tamed the traditional vindaloo heat. Add more cayenne if a tongue lashing is your pleasure.

With its luxurious coconut milk sauce, this dish is terrific over basmati rice. For a variation using lamb, see below.

20 MINUTES HIGH PRESSURE

1 to 2 tablespoons vegetable oil or ghee (clarified butter, page 237)

1 large onion, peeled, halved, and thinly sliced

2 pounds boneless pork shoulder (butt) or loin, cut into 1-inch cubes, and well trimmed

2 teaspoons whole cumin seeds

¼ cup water

One 14-ounce can unsweetened coconut milk

2 tablespoons coarse-grained mustard (such as Maille old-style Dijon), or more to taste

1 teaspoon salt, or to taste

1 teaspoon turmeric

¼ teaspoon cayenne, or more to taste

Two 10-ounce packages frozen chopped spinach

1½ pounds Yukon Gold potatoes, peeled and cut into 2-inch chunks

Over medium-high heat, heat 1 tablespoon of oil in the cooker. Cook the onion, stirring frequently, for 2 minutes. Add the pork, cumin seeds, and more oil if needed, and cook until the pork loses its pink color, stirring frequently, 2 to 3 minutes. Add the water and stir well, taking care to scrape up any browned bits stuck to the bottom of the cooker. Add the coconut milk and blend in the mustard, salt, turmeric, and cayenne. Add the frozen blocks of spinach and set the potatoes on top.

Lock the lid in place. Over high heat, bring to high pressure. Lower the heat to maintain high pressure and cook for 20 minutes. Quick-release the pressure. Remove the lid, tilting it away from you to allow any excess steam to escape.

If you wish, slash the potatoes into bite-sized pieces. Stir the vindaloo well, and add more cayenne, mustard, and salt, if needed.

SERVES 4

LAMB VINDALOO

Substitute cubed lamb shoulder or leg for the pork. Cooking time under pressure remains the same.

SWEET AND SOUR RED CABBAGE WITH PORK

Red cabbage has such a remarkable color, I can't imagine why it's not the focus of more still-life paintings. Art history aside, it's a boon that we cooks can enjoy its beauty and taste in this traditional recipe.

10 MINUTES HIGH PRESSURE

2 tablespoons butter or vegetable oil

2 cups coarsely chopped onions

1/2 cup chicken broth or water

1 tablespoon Dijon mustard

1 teaspoon salt, or to taste

1/4 teaspoon ground allspice

2 pounds pork shoulder (butt) or loin, cut into 1 1/2-inch chunks and well trimmed

1/3 cup dark or yellow raisins or chopped, dried apricots

2 pounds red cabbage, quartered, cored, and cut into 1/2-inch slices crosswise (see Tip)

3 tablespoons apple cider vinegar, or more to taste

1 cup applesauce, preferably unsweetened

2 pounds Yukon Gold potatoes, peeled and cut into 1 1/2-inch chunks

Pinch of sugar (optional)

Over medium-high heat, heat the butter in the cooker. Cook the onions, stirring frequently, until lightly browned, 4 to 5 minutes. Add the broth, mustard, salt, allspice, pork, and raisins. Place one-third of the cabbage on top and sprinkle with 1 tablespoon vinegar. Repeat with two more layers of cabbage, sprinkling each layer with vinegar. Pour on the applesauce and set the potatoes on top. (Don't be concerned that the cooker is quite full; the cabbage will wilt as the pressure rises.)

Lock the lid in place. Over high heat, bring to high pressure. Reduce the heat just enough to maintain high pressure and cook for 10 minutes. Quick-release the pressure. Remove the lid, tilting it away from you to allow excess steam to escape.

If you wish, slice the potatoes into smaller pieces (you can do this right in the cooker) and stir them into the stew. If necessary, adjust the seasonings to achieve a good sweet-sour balance, adding a bit more vinegar and salt and a pinch of sugar. If the potatoes or pork are not quite tender, cover and simmer over medium heat until done.

SERVES 4 TO 6

TIP
Sometimes cooking transforms the color of red cabbage to a purplish blue. Marvel and enjoy.

PORTUGUESE RED BEANS WITH SAUSAGE AND KALE

This soupy stew is reminiscent of the great Portuguese sopa de pedra. The pedras (stones) are a reference to the gleaming mahogany kidney beans at the heart of this dish. Sausage and browned garlic add lusty flavor, and a generous portion of kale lightens up this hearty meal in a bowl.

It's quite substantial on its own, and also nice served over bulgur. Leftovers will get quite thick; serve as is or thin with chicken broth.

For a quick, impromptu version that uses potatoes instead of beans, see the variation on page 119.

12 MINUTES HIGH PRESSURE

2 TO 3 MINUTES ADDITIONAL COOKING

1 ½ cups red kidney beans, picked over and rinsed, soaked overnight in ample water to cover or speed-soaked (page 24)

2 tablespoons olive oil

2 tablespoons thinly sliced garlic

2 cups coarsely chopped onions

3 ½ cups water

½ pound linguiça, chorizo, or other spicy, smoked sausage, diced

2 large bay leaves

1 pound kale, stems thinly sliced, leaves coarsely chopped, thoroughly rinsed

One 15-ounce can diced tomatoes or peeled plum tomatoes, coarsely chopped, with liquid

Salt and freshly ground pepper to taste

Tabasco sauce to taste

Drain the beans and set aside. Over medium-high heat, heat the oil in the cooker. Add the garlic and cook, stirring constantly, until lightly browned, about 1 minute. Add the onions and cook over medium heat, stirring frequently, until fairly soft, about 5 minutes. Transfer the mixture to a bowl and set aside.

Add the water and scrape up any browned bits sticking to the bottom of the cooker. Add the reserved beans, sausage, bay leaves, and kale. (Don't be concerned that the cooker will be quite full; the kale will shrink dramatically as the cooker comes up to pressure.) Pour the tomatoes on top. *Do not stir.*

Lock the lid in place. Over high heat, bring to high pressure. Lower the heat to maintain high pressure and cook for 12 minutes. Reduce the pressure with a quick-release method. Remove the lid, tilting it away from you to allow any excess steam to escape. If the beans are not tender, return to high pressure for 3 to 5 minutes more.

Stir well and discard the bay leaves. Add the reserved onion-garlic mixture, salt, pepper, and Tabasco sauce. Cook until the garlic flavor suffuses the dish, 2 to 3 minutes.

SERVES 4

POTATOES WITH SAUSAGE AND KALE

Omit the beans. Use 3 cups chicken or turkey broth instead of the water. Add 2 pounds red-skinned potatoes, scrubbed and cut into 1-inch chunks, after you add the broth. Proceed as directed, but reduce cooking time to 4 minutes under high pressure. Stir well so that potatoes break up slightly to thicken the stew. Season to taste.

VEGETARIAN VERSION

Use vegetable broth instead of water and omit the sausage. Stir in a few drops of liquid smoke at the end, if you wish.

LOUISIANA BLACK-EYED PEAS WITH ANDOUILLE AND COLLARDS

Since they require no presoaking, black-eyed peas are a good choice for last-minute suppers. In this stew, they provide a mild, earthy backdrop for a chile-hot sausage like andouille. A half pound of sausage flavors the peas nicely, but you can double the amount if you're a sausage lover. (However, if you're using real Cajun andouille sausage, proceed with caution as it can be very hot.)

Since the collards turn olive green under pressure, I like to brighten up the dish with diced, roasted red peppers and a sprinkling of fresh parsley. It's ideal to serve the stew on rice and, by all means, pass the Tabasco.

10 MINUTES HIGH PRESSURE

3 MINUTES ADDITIONAL COOKING

1 pound collard greens

1/2 to 1 pound andouille or other spicy smoked sausage, cut into 1/2-inch slices

2 to 3 teaspoons olive oil (optional)

1 1/2 cups coarsely chopped onions

4 cups water

2 cups black-eyed peas, picked over and rinsed

2 large bay leaves

2 teaspoons sweet paprika

2 large ribs celery, coarsely chopped

2 large cloves garlic, pushed through a press

1/2 teaspoon dried thyme leaves

Salt and freshly ground black pepper to taste

2 to 3 tablespoons apple cider vinegar

2 large red bell peppers, roasted (page 241), seeded, and cut into 1/2-inch squares

Chopped fresh parsley, for garnish

Hold the collards in a bunch on a chopping board. Trim off and discard the bottom inch or so of the stems. Thinly slice the stems. Stack 3 or 4 of the leaves and cut into thirds lengthwise. Cut as thinly as possible crosswise. Repeat with the remaining leaves. Swish the chopped collards in a large bowl of water. Drain in a large colander and set aside.

Lightly brown the sausage in the cooker, about 1 minute on each side. Add oil, if needed, to prevent sticking. Add the onions and cook, stirring constantly, 1 minute. Add the water and scrape up any browned bits sticking to the bottom of the cooker. Add the black-eyed peas, bay leaves, and paprika. Set the celery and collards on top. (Don't be concerned that the cooker will be filled beyond the recommended maximum capacity; the collards will shrink dramatically as the cooker comes up to pressure.)

Lock the lid in place. Over high heat, bring to high pressure. Lower the heat to maintain high pressure and cook for 10 minutes. Quick-release the pressure by setting the cooker under cold running water. Remove the lid, tilting it away from you to allow excess steam to escape.

Stir the stew well to distribute the collards. Add ½ cup water if the mixture seems dry. Remove the bay leaves and add the garlic, thyme, salt, and pepper. Perk up the flavors with vinegar and simmer, uncovered, over medium heat until the black-eyed peas are tender and the garlic loses its raw taste, about 3 minutes. Stir in the roasted red pepper. Garnish the serving bowl or individual portions with parsley.

SERVES 4 ON ITS OWN OR 6 OVER RICE

LAMB

LAMB UNDER PRESSURE

Lamb has never been as popular as beef in America, but those who love it are wildly enthusiastic about its rich taste. Indeed, lamb's flavor is so intense that a small amount of meat infuses a dish with its distinctive taste, as you will see in the recipe for the Tunisian Vegetable Ragout. Lamb stews become very full flavored without your going to the trouble of browning the meat, but if you'd like the meat to have richer color, by all means brown it in batches before you proceed with the recipes.

When buying lamb, look for light red meat with white and firm surface fat. There should be some red visible in the bones; bleached-out white bones indicate that the meat is old. Once purchased, lamb can be stored in the refrigerator for up to 5 days or until the expiration date on the package, whichever comes first.

Most of the recipes call for lamb shoulder or leg, which can be used interchangeably, depending upon price, availability, and your personal preference. The best choice is shoulder, which has a luscious texture and becomes fork tender in 20 minutes or less. If you have trouble finding cubed, boneless shoulder, opt for shoulder chops and cut the meat into pieces yourself—an easy task. Buy about 30 percent more to account for the weight of the bones, and include the bones in the stew for added flavor.

If you go to a butcher, he may try to talk you into buying leg instead of shoulder. Leg can more easily be cut into neat cubes, affording him greater profit for less work. You'll get a tasty stew using leg, but it is a leaner piece of meat and can be slightly dry and stringy. Some people actually prefer it, and if you're counting your fat grams, this is the cut for you.

If you're in the supermarket and see a package of cubed lamb labeled "stew meat," it is likely to be shoulder or leg—or a combination. To assure more even cooking, you can buy a section of boned leg and cube the meat yourself—again a simple task. Figure that a 3½-pound piece of leg will yield 2 pounds of trimmed, cubed meat. (Yes, there is a surprising amount lost in trimming.)

The recipe for Scotch Broth calls for lamb's neck, a very economical cut that is always full of flavor. Unfortunately, it's also full of fat, so you always need to degrease the stew before serving. However, once you've tried the Scotch Broth, if you like lamb neck, you can substitute it in the other recipes. Just increase the amount by 50 percent to accommodate for the weight of the bones. Usually the pieces of lamb neck vary in size from 2 to 3 inches; don't be concerned, as they'll cook evenly. After cooking, you can either chop the meat and discard the bones or serve the stew, bones and all.

SCOTCH BROTH REVISITED

I've lightened up the traditional version of this hearty winter soup by preparing it in two phases. First, I cook the lamb and barley with vegetables to create a rich broth, making a special point of degreasing the broth before adding leeks and additional vegetables for a final few minutes of cooking. (The degreasing can either be done by setting the broth in the refrigerator overnight or by using a gravy separator.) This approach gives the soup a fresh taste, and frozen peas tossed in at the last minute brighten up the appearance.

Lamb neck—the traditional cut used for this stew—is delicious, economical, and readily available, but quite fatty. Once you've discarded the bones and gristle, you'll end up with only about a cupful of meat, but the main "work" of the lamb neck is to create a deeply flavored broth.

To cut down on prep time, bring the lamb and water to the boil as you prepare and add the remaining vegetables.

20 MINUTES HIGH PRESSURE (BROTH)

4 MINUTES HIGH PRESSURE (VEGETABLES)

1 MINUTE ADDITIONAL COOKING

2½ to 3 pounds lamb neck, trimmed of surface fat, and cut into 2-inch chunks (approximately)

8 cups cold water

2 teaspoons salt, or to taste

1 large onion, peeled and quartered

2 large ribs celery, halved crosswise

2 large carrots, peeled and halved crosswise

2 large bay leaves

A few leek greens (optional), plus 1½ cups thinly sliced leeks (white and light green part only)

Small bunch parsley stems, tied with kitchen string

½ cup pearl barley

1 tablespoon butter or vegetable oil

2 pounds rutabaga, peeled and cut into ½-inch chunks, or purple-topped turnips, peeled and cut into 1-inch chunks

2 large carrots or parsnips, peeled and cut into 1-inch chunks

continued

½ cup red lentils, picked over and rinsed

Freshly ground black pepper to taste

1 cup frozen peas (rinse off any ice crystals)

3 to 4 tablespoons chopped fresh parsley, for garnish

Rinse the lamb and set it in the cooker with the water. Over medium-high heat, bring to a boil. Skim off any scum that forms on the surface. Add 1 teaspoon of salt, return to a rapid boil over high heat, and skim again. Add the onion, celery, carrots, bay leaves, leek greens, if using, parsley stems, and barley.

Lock the lid in place. Over high heat, bring to high pressure. Reduce the heat just enough to maintain high pressure and cook for 20 minutes. Quick-release the pressure by setting the cooker under cold running water. Remove the lid, tilting it away from you to allow excess steam to escape.

Allow the soup to cool slightly. Pour it through a colander set over a large bowl or storage container. Discard the vegetables, bay leaves, and any loose lamb bones. (You may, if you wish, separate all of the meat from the bones, chop it, and discard all of the bones.)

If serving right away, set the lamb and barley aside and degrease the broth using a gravy separator. Otherwise, set the broth in one container and the lamb and barley in another and refrigerate overnight. The following day, remove the fat that congeals on the broth's surface.

Rinse out the cooker. Heat the butter over medium-high heat until it begins to foam. Add the sliced leeks and cook for 1 minute, stirring frequently. Add the defatted lamb broth, rutabaga, carrots, red lentils, remaining teaspoon of salt, and the pepper.

Lock the lid in place. Over high heat, bring to high pressure. Reduce the heat just enough to maintain high pressure and cook for 4 minutes. Quick-release the pressure. If the vegetables are not quite tender, set (but do not lock) the lid in place and cook them over medium heat at a gentle boil until done.

Stir in the lamb and barley and cook until thoroughly heated. Adjust seasonings. Stir in the peas and cook until tender, about 1 minute more. Serve in large soup bowls, garnished with a sprinkling of parsley.

SERVES 6

RISOTTO WITH LAMB SHANKS

Elizabeth Germain, a talented Boston-based chef who loves both lamb and the pressure cooker, shared with me her terrific recipe for lamb shanks with risotto. Her inspiration was the classic Italian osso buco *(veal shanks) served with risotto Milanese and topped with a minced parsley-lemon-garlic mixture known as* gremolata.

First, the shanks are cooked and then the diced meat is cooked again, along with the risotto. This approach uniformly tenderizes any "tough spots" in the cooked shank meat and infuses the rice with superb flavor. You can streamline preparation by chopping the celery and carrots and preparing the gremolata while the shanks are cooking.

This is an elegant risotto, ideal for celebrating a special occasion—or just plain celebrating life itself.

20 MINUTES HIGH PRESSURE PLUS 10-MINUTE NATURAL PRESSURE RELEASE (LAMB)

4 MINUTES HIGH PRESSURE (RISOTTO)

3 TO 4 MINUTES ADDITIONAL COOKING

1 tablespoon olive oil

¾ cup chopped shallots

¾ cup thinly sliced leeks

1 cup dry white wine

2 to 2½ cups chicken broth

1 tablespoon tomato paste

1 tablespoon fresh thyme leaves or 1 teaspoon dried

1 teaspoon salt, or to taste

2 large bay leaves

3 lamb shanks (3½ to 4 pounds total), well trimmed (see Tip)

1 cup diced carrots

1 cup diced celery

1½ cups arborio rice

½ cup freshly grated Parmesan or Pecorino Romano cheese

continued

GREMOLATA

¼ cup minced fresh parsley

1 tablespoon lemon zest (from 2 large lemons)

1 teaspoon minced garlic (optional: for raw garlic lovers only)

Heat the oil in the cooker over medium-high heat. Cook the shallots and leeks, stirring frequently, until slightly softened, about 2 minutes. Add the wine, bring to a boil, and cook until reduced by half, 2 to 3 minutes. Add 2 cups of the broth and blend in the tomato paste. Add the thyme, salt, and bay leaves. Arrange the shanks so that most or all of the fleshy parts are submerged in the broth.

Lock the lid in place. Over high heat, bring to high pressure. Reduce the heat just enough to maintain high pressure and cook for 20 minutes. Allow the pressure to come down naturally for 10 minutes. Quick-release any remaining pressure. Remove the lid, tilting it away from you to allow excess steam to escape.

Transfer the shanks to a cutting board. Discard the bay leaves. If the broth seems fatty, degrease it using a gravy separator. Measure the lamb broth and vegetables and add as much of the remaining chicken broth as needed to equal a total of 4 cups. Return the broth and vegetables to the cooker.

When the shanks are cool enough to handle, slice the meat from the bone and cut it into bite-sized pieces—or large chunks, if you prefer. (If the lamb is already very tender, you can set it aside while cooking the rice and stir it in at the end.) Add the lamb, carrots, celery, and rice to the broth. Lock the lid in place. Over high heat, bring to high pressure. Reduce the heat just enough to maintain high pressure and cook for 4 minutes. Quick-release the pressure under cold running water. Remove the lid, tilting it away from you to allow excess steam to escape.

Boil over medium-high heat, stirring constantly, until the rice is tender but still chewy and the risotto loses most of its soupiness and becomes creamy and thick, 3 to 4 minutes. Turn off the heat and stir in the cheese.

In a small bowl, prepare the gremolata by tossing together the parsley, lemon zest, and garlic, if using. Sprinkle a heaping tablespoon of gremolata over each portion and serve immediately.

SERVES 4

TIP

It can sometimes be difficult to find lamb shanks of equal size. As long as the shanks are less than 1½ pounds each, you'll be fine. The final cooking period with the rice takes care of any pieces of meat that are still a bit tough.

GREEK LAMB WITH POTATOES AND OLIVES

The simple foods of the Greek kitchen often don't travel well, dependent as they are on top-quality ingredients, clear blue skies, and the casual atmosphere of a taverna. But this dish has made the journey quite successfully.

If you can find those gorgeous mahogany kalamata olives, so much the better. But any full-flavored brined olive will do. Don't add salt until the end, when you determine how much the olives have seasoned the stew.

The deep brown sauce is extremely flavorful but thin, so serve the dish in large soup bowls and pass some hearty peasant bread for sopping it up. Or, if you prefer, mash a few of the potatoes against the side of the cooker to thicken the stew.

16 TO 20 MINUTES HIGH PRESSURE

1 tablespoon olive oil

1 cup thinly sliced leeks or coarsely chopped onions

2 pounds boneless lamb shoulder or leg, cut into 1 1/2-inch chunks, well trimmed

1/2 cup dry red wine

2 large ribs celery, cut into 1-inch chunks

3/4 cup Greek olives (pitted, if you wish)

2 teaspoons dried oregano leaves

1/4 teaspoon crushed red pepper flakes, or more to taste

One 15-ounce can diced tomatoes or plum tomatoes, coarsely chopped, with liquid

2 1/2 pounds Yukon Gold potatoes, peeled and cut into 2-inch chunks

Salt and freshly ground black pepper to taste

1/4 cup finely chopped fresh parsley, for garnish

Heat the oil over medium-high heat. Add the leeks and cook, stirring frequently, until they begin to soften, about 3 minutes. Add the lamb and cook, stirring frequently, until the lamb is no longer pink, about 3 minutes more. Stir in the wine and cook over high heat until the wine has reduced by half, about 2 minutes. Stir in the celery, olives, oregano, and crushed red pepper. Pour on the tomatoes. *Do not stir.* Set the potatoes on top.

Lock the lid in place. Over high heat, bring to high pressure. Lower the heat just enough to maintain high pressure and cook for 16 minutes. Quick-release the pressure. Remove the lid, tilting it away from you to allow any excess steam to escape. Remove the potatoes and divide them among 4 large bowls or deep plates. If the lamb is not sufficiently tender, return to high pressure for 4 minutes more.

Stir the stew well. Add salt, pepper, and additional crushed red pepper, if needed. Ladle the stew on top of the potatoes and garnish with parsley.

SERVES 4

IRISH LAMB STEW

Omit the olive oil and heat 3 strips of chopped bacon in the cooker until it renders a thin film of fat. Add 2 cups sliced leeks or chopped onions and cook, stirring frequently, for 3 minutes. Use 1 cup of water instead of wine and don't bother to reduce it. Omit the celery, olives, oregano, and red pepper and substitute 1 teaspoon each dried thyme leaves and salt. Omit the tomatoes and set 4 large peeled carrots (halved crosswise, if necessary, to fit in the cooker) on top of the potatoes. Proceed as directed in the recipe.

(Note: This variation is for nostalgic Irish folks and those in the mood for a down-home, straightforward stew. If you're looking for pizzazz, stick with the Greek version.)

LAMB WITH APRICOTS, PRUNES, AND MINT

This quick but memorable stew comes from the Moroccan kitchen, where dried fruits and lamb are often joined in the cooking pot. The fruits soften to create a luscious, sweet, thick sauce. The potatoes are cooked in large pieces, then chopped and stirred into the stew at the end, along with a flavor-packed trio of garlic, mint, and lemon zest. It's worth going out of your way for fresh mint: It really brings this dish alive.

For a nice change, instead of chopping the potatoes, you can make a bed of thickly sliced potatoes and spoon the stew on top.

16 MINUTES HIGH PRESSURE

2 MINUTES ADDITIONAL COOKING

½ cup dry white wine or vermouth

½ cup water

2 cups coarsely chopped onions

1 cup dried apricots

½ cup pitted prunes

1 teaspoon salt, or to taste

⅛ teaspoon ground cinnamon

2 pounds boneless lamb shoulder or leg, cut into 1½-inch cubes, well trimmed

2½ pounds Yukon Gold or red-skinned potatoes, cut into 2-inch chunks (peeling optional)

1 small clove garlic, pushed through a press

½ cup loosely packed fresh mint leaves, chopped, or 2 to 3 teaspoons dried mint

1 tablespoon lemon zest (from 2 large lemons)

Set the first 8 ingredients in the cooker and stir. Set the potatoes on top.

Lock the lid in place. Over high heat, bring to high pressure. Lower the heat to maintain high pressure and cook for 16 minutes. Quick-release the pressure. Remove the lid, tilting it away from you to allow any excess steam to escape. If the lamb is not fork tender, remove the potatoes and return to high pressure for 4 minutes more.

Chop the potatoes, if you wish. Add the garlic and cook over medium heat, stirring to coarsely puree the fruits and create a thick sauce. A few minutes before serving, stir the mint and lemon zest into the stew and simmer over medium heat until the flavors mingle slightly and the garlic has lost its raw taste, about 2 minutes. Adjust the seasonings before serving.

SERVES 4

VARIATIONS

Substitute orange for lemon zest.

Instead of ½ cup chopped fresh mint, use ¼ cup fresh mint and ¼ cup fresh cilantro or parsley.

TUNISIAN VEGETABLE RAGOUT WITH LAMB

Since I began cooking under pressure in the late eighties, I've felt fortunate to have the enthusiastic support of my colleague Paula Wolfert, who travels the world in search of authentic recipes from the best home cooks. "All over the Mediterranean and North Africa, everyone relies on the pressure cooker to make soups and stews," Paula has reported to me on numerous occasions.

In this recipe, I've created a pressure-cooked version of a rustic lamb stew from Paula's Mediterranean Cooking. The dish is chock-full of earthy ingredients, including chickpeas, turnips, Swiss chard, and spinach. The greens cook down into a thick, savory sauce enriched by the lamb juices. Instead of cooking a generous amount of parsley along with the stew as in Paula's recipe, I stir in the parsley and some fresh lemon juice at the end to give the dish a lively finish.

The ragout is good on its own or over couscous or bulgur. Leftovers are tasty when tossed right into the grains, with an extra drizzle of lemon juice.

16 MINUTES HIGH PRESSURE

8 TO 9 MINUTES ADDITIONAL COOKING

1 cup chickpeas, picked over and rinsed, soaked overnight in ample water to cover or speed-soaked (page 24)

1 tablespoon olive oil

3 scallions, thinly sliced (keep white and green parts separate)

1 pound lamb shoulder chops, cut into ½-inch pieces, well trimmed (see Tip)

2 tablespoons tomato paste

1 cup water, or more if needed

¼ teaspoon crushed red pepper flakes, or more to taste

1 pound Swiss chard, stems thinly sliced, leaves coarsely chopped (keep stems and leaves separate)

Salt and freshly ground black pepper

1½ pounds purple-topped turnips, peeled and cut into ½-inch dice

10 ounces triple-washed spinach, chopped, or ¾ pound untrimmed spinach, trimmed, washed, and chopped

¾ cup tightly packed parsley leaves (no need to chop)

2 tablespoons freshly squeezed lemon juice, or more to taste

Drain and rinse the chickpeas. Set aside.

Heat the oil in the cooker over medium-high heat. Cook the sliced scallion bulbs and lamb, stirring almost constantly, until the lamb is no longer pink, about 3 minutes. Add the tomato paste and stir constantly until it glistens and coats the meat, 2 minutes more. (If the mixture begins to burn, immediately add water as directed in the next paragraph.)

Add the water and red pepper flakes. Stir well to loosen up any browned bits that have stuck to the bottom of the cooker. Push the lamb aside and add the reserved chickpeas. Arrange the ingredients so that all or most of the chickpeas are either in the water or under the lamb. Scatter the chard stems and half the chard leaves on top.

Lock the lid in place. Over high heat, bring to high pressure. Lower the heat to maintain high pressure and cook for 16 minutes. Quick-release the pressure. Remove the lid, tilting it away from you to allow excess steam to escape. If the chickpea mixture is dry, stir in ½ cup of water. If the lamb or chickpeas is not sufficiently tender, return to high pressure for 5 minutes more or cover and cook over medium heat until done.

Add salt and pepper to taste. Stir in the turnips and remaining Swiss chard leaves, cover, and cook over medium heat until the turnips begin to soften, about 5 minutes. Stir in the spinach and scallion greens and continue cooking, covered, until the turnips are tender but still firm, 2 to 3 minutes more.

Stir in the parsley and cook until it wilts, about 1 minute. Add enough lemon juice to give the ragout a distinct citric edge. Add more salt and pepper, if needed.

SERVES 4

TIP

Don't be concerned about cutting every last bit of meat from the bones. Include the bones for added flavor during cooking. Cut off any cooked meat and discard the bones before serving.

VEGETARIAN VERSION

Omit the lamb and cook the scallion bulbs in the oil for 1 minute. Add the tomato paste and proceed as directed

VEAL

VEAL UNDER PRESSURE

Veal is a delightful meat to cook, with its delicate flavor and reliable tenderness. However, because of its light color and mild taste, browning is usually essential for a successful final dish.

Depending upon how it's dead, raw veal ranges in color from reddish to light pink to grayish white. The meat has a relatively high moisture content and does not keep well. Be sure to cook it by the expiration date or within two days of purchase, whichever comes first.

Avoid freezing veal if you can. While other raw meats freeze reasonably well, when veal is frozen its thin cell walls rupture and a good deal of the juices are lost as the meat thaws. The higher moisture content makes it more difficult to brown since the veal tends to steam in its own juices. To facilitate browning of defrosted veal, wrap the cubes in a clean kitchen towel and press gently to release excess moisture.

With the exception of shanks and a whole boneless shoulder roast, which are considered prize cuts, the remaining recipes in this section call for more moderately priced cubed veal shoulder. I've also had fine results using what the supermarket labeled "veal stew meat," which is commonly boneless meat from the shoulder and neck. When you're lucky enough to find healthy-looking cubed veal on sale, you'll find the price comparable to boneless chicken breast. Figure on ½ pound per person since veal shrinks about 30 percent as it cooks.

If you happen to see a boneless shoulder roast on sale, grab it and cut it into cubes yourself, thus assuring that the meat will come from the same part of the animal and cook uniformly. When nothing else is available, buy veal shoulder round or blade chops (even if they are less than 1-inch thick) and cut them into cubes as best you can, leaving some meat attached to the bone. Cut the meat from the bone after cooking. Since a 1-pound chop yields only 10 to 12 ounces of meat, you'll need to buy about 3 pounds of chops for a recipe that calls for 2 pounds of veal. But you'll have the bonus of some veal bones to enrich the stew.

VEAL POT ROAST WITH POLENTA AND BASIL

Greg Mowery, a passionate New York cook, approached me at a party to "talk pressure cookers." He reported with considerable enthusiasm that veal shoulder roast is one of the best things he has ever made in the cooker. I tried out his recipe and concluded that he was right.

After the veal is cooked, the strained, flavorful broth is used as the base for "instant" polenta, a delicious cornmeal porridge made from a boxed product called quick-cooking polenta. (You'll find it in supermarkets and gourmet shops.) The sliced veal is set on top of the polenta and then sauced with basil-flecked mushrooms and tomatoes. A royal feast.

It's rare to find a veal roast in most supermarkets, so you may have to order it from a butcher. You may use either the boneless shoulder clod or the chuck, a fattier section of the shoulder that some people find more flavorful.

For a version of this recipe using mashed potatoes instead of polenta, see page 141.

45 MINUTES HIGH PRESSURE PLUS 10-MINUTE NATURAL PRESSURE RELEASE (VEAL ROAST)

3 TO 5 MINUTES ADDITIONAL COOKING

2 to 3 tablespoons olive oil

3 pounds boneless veal shoulder roast, well trimmed (see Tip)

2 cups coarsely chopped onions

1 pound cremini or button mushrooms (or a mixture), trimmed and halved

2 tablespoons coarsely chopped garlic

1/2 cup dry red or white wine or vermouth

1 1/2 cups veal or chicken broth

2 teaspoons Italian herb blend (page 238 or store-bought)

1 teaspoon salt, or to taste

Freshly ground black pepper to taste

One 35-ounce can peeled tomatoes, with liquid

1/2 cup loosely packed chopped fresh basil

continued

1 ½ to 2 cups quick-cooking polenta

½ cup freshly grated Parmesan cheese

Over medium-high heat, heat 1 tablespoon of oil in the cooker. Brown the roast well, rotating every 2 or 3 minutes, and adding more oil as needed, about 12 minutes total. Set the roast aside in a large bowl.

Add the onions and mushrooms and cook, stirring frequently, until the onions soften slightly and the mushrooms begin to give up their liquid, about 3 minutes. Add the garlic and cook for an additional minute, stirring frequently. Add the wine and stir well, taking care to scrape up any browned bits stuck to the bottom of the cooker. Cook over high heat until about half of the wine evaporates, 1 to 2 minutes. Add the broth, herbs, salt, and pepper. Set the veal roast in the liquid. Pour the canned tomatoes over the roast. *Do not stir.*

Lock the lid in place. Over high heat, bring to high pressure. Lower the heat, to maintain high pressure and cook for 45 minutes. Let the pressure drop naturally for 10 minutes. Quick-release any remaining pressure. Remove the lid, tilting it away from you to allow any excess steam to escape.

Remove the roast and set it on a carving board. Pour the sauce through a large strainer. Place the tomatoes and vegetables in a bowl. Break up any whole tomatoes and stir in the basil. Cover with foil or plastic wrap and set aside.

Measure the broth and pour it back into the cooker. Set aside ¼ cup of polenta per cup of liquid. (In other words, for 6 cups of broth, measure out 1½ cups of polenta.) Bring the broth to a boil. Gradually sprinkle the polenta into the liquid, whisking vigorously to prevent lumps. Reduce the heat to medium and cook with the lid set (but not locked) in place, whisking occasionally, until the polenta develops the consistency of a thick porridge, 3 to 5 minutes. Season with salt and pepper to taste.

While the polenta is cooking, remove any strings and carve the roast into ½-inch slices. Divide the cooked polenta among 6 large, shallow soup bowls or deep plates. Sprinkle a generous tablespoon of the Parmesan over each portion, then set the veal on the polenta. Spoon the vegetables on top and serve.

SERVES 6

VEAL ROAST WITH PARMESAN MASHED POTATOES

Cook the roast as directed, and follow the instructions through the sentence that reads "Cover with foil or plastic wrap and set aside."

Return the broth to the cooker. Omit the polenta and add 3 pounds peeled russet potatoes, cut into 1½-inch chunks. Cook under pressure for 6 minutes. While the potatoes are cooking, carve the veal into ½-inch slices.

Quick-release the pressure. Remove the lid, tilting it away from you to allow any excess steam to escape. Remove the potatoes with a slotted spoon and transfer to a large bowl. Return the tomato-mushroom mixture and sliced veal to the broth and reheat. Mash the potatoes with a ricer, adding 2 tablespoons olive oil, the Parmesan, and enough broth to flavor and moisten the potatoes. Add salt and pepper to taste.

Set a mound of mashed potatoes on each of 6 plates and arrange slices of veal against each mound. Lift the vegetables out of the broth with a slotted spoon and scatter them on top of the veal and potatoes. Season the remaining broth (and any remaining vegetables) with salt and pepper and pass it in a sauceboat.

VEAL STEW WITH CAULIFLOWER

This elegant and delicately flavored stew is a pressure-cooker version of a recipe in Marcella Hazan's Marcella Cucina. *After cooking the veal, add cauliflower florets and braise them just until barely tender.*

Stir in a touch of heavy cream at the end to enrich the thin, wine-infused broth. Since the wine's flavor predominates, be sure to use one whose taste you enjoy.

The stew can be served on its own, but rice complements it nicely.

12 MINUTES HIGH PRESSURE

6 TO 10 MINUTES ADDITIONAL COOKING

1 to 2 tablespoons olive oil

2½ pounds boneless veal shoulder, cut into 1-inch cubes, well trimmed

1 tablespoon butter

1 cup finely chopped onions

2 teaspoons chopped garlic

2½ teaspoons dried rosemary leaves, broken into bits

2½ teaspoons fennel seeds

½ teaspoon salt, or to taste

Freshly ground black pepper

¾ cup dry white wine

2 large plum tomatoes, seeded and finely chopped (about ¾ cup)

1 medium head (about 2¼ pounds) cauliflower, trimmed and cut into small florets (about 1½ inches across the top)

¼ cup heavy cream

2 tablespoons chopped fresh parsley, for garnish

Heat 1 tablespoon of oil in the cooker over medium-high heat. Brown the veal in 4 batches, 4 to 6 minutes per batch, adding more oil if needed. Reserve the browned veal on a platter and set aside.

Heat the butter in the cooker. Cook the onions, garlic, rosemary, and fennel seeds over medium-high heat, stirring frequently, until the onions are slightly softened, about 3 minutes. Stir in the salt and pepper. Add the wine and cook over high heat, stirring vigorously and scraping up any browned bits sticking to the bottom of the cooker. Continue cooking at a rapid boil until the wine is slightly reduced, 1 to 2 minutes. Add the reserved veal and accumulated juices.

Lock the lid in place. Over high heat, bring to high pressure. Reduce the heat just enough to maintain high pressure and cook for 12 minutes. Quick-release the pressure. Remove the lid, tilting it away from you to allow excess steam to escape.

Stir in the tomatoes and cauliflower. Set (but do not lock) the lid in place and cook over medium heat at a gentle boil, stirring occasionally, until the cauliflower is tender but still firm, 6 to 10 minutes. Stir in the heavy cream and add salt to taste. Garnish individual servings with the parsley.

SERVES 4

SYRIAN VEAL STEW WITH BLACK-EYED PEAS

In his fascinating book, The World of Jewish Cooking, *chef and rabbi Gil Marks claims that Syrian Jews reserve this fragrantly spiced dish for the Sabbath and special festival meals. I was immediately drawn to adapting this unusual recipe since I love the earthy taste of black-eyed peas, a quick-cooking legume that doesn't require presoaking and cooks in the same amount of time as veal.*

I've added diced dried apricots and currants to Rabbi Marks' recipe. These fruits provide a nice complement to the spices and add texture and punches of flavor to this comforting dish.

This stew is filling enough to serve on its own, but becomes more festive when served over rice cooked with with a pinch of saffron or ground cardamom.

12 MINUTES HIGH PRESSURE

2 TO 3 MINUTES ADDITIONAL COOKING

2 to 3 tablespoons olive oil
2 pounds boneless veal shoulder, cut into 1-inch cubes, well trimmed
1 1/2 cups coarsely chopped onions
4 cups veal or chicken broth
2 cups black-eyed peas, picked over and rinsed
1/2 teaspoon ground allspice, or more to taste
1/2 teaspoon ground cinnamon
1 pound carrots, peeled and halved crosswise
1/2 cup dried apricots, each snipped into 4 pieces
1/4 cup dried currants
1/2 cup minced fresh parsley, plus 2 tablespoons, for garnish
1 teaspoon salt, or to taste
Freshly ground black pepper to taste

Heat 1 tablespoon of oil in the cooker over medium-high heat. Brown the veal in 4 batches, 4 to 6 minutes per batch, adding oil as needed. Set the browned veal aside. Add the onions and cook, stirring frequently, until lightly browned, about 5 minutes. Transfer the onions to a small bowl and set aside.

Add the broth and stir well to scrape up any browned bits sticking to the bottom of the cooker. Add the black-eyed peas and browned veal along with any accumulated juices. Stir in the allspice and cinnamon. Set the carrots on top.

Lock the lid in place. Over high heat, bring to high pressure. Reduce the heat just enough to maintain high pressure and cook for 12 minutes. Quick-release the pressure. Remove the lid, tilting it away from you to allow excess steam to escape.

Stir in ½ cup of water if the mixture seems dry. Add the reserved onions, apricots, currants, ½ cup of parsley, additional allspice if needed, and salt and pepper. Cook over medium heat just until the dried fruits plump up a bit, 2 to 3 minutes. Garnish individual servings with parsley.

SERVES 4 BY ITSELF OR 6 OVER RICE

VEAL WITH OLIVES AND ARTICHOKE HEARTS

The subtle flavor of veal and artichoke hearts is enhanced when mingled with a quality pasta sauce and the salty essence of olives.

Delicious as it is, the finished dish is pale unless you brighten it up with a parsley garnish. I recommend serving this stew over rice.

12 MINUTES HIGH PRESSURE

2 to 3 tablespoons olive oil

2 pounds boneless veal shoulder, cut into 1-inch cubes, well trimmed

1/2 cup dry white wine

1 1/2 cups thinly sliced leeks or coarsely chopped onions

1 cup veal or chicken broth

4 large ribs celery, cut into 3/4-inch chunks

1/2 cup niçoise or other Mediterranean black olives (pitting optional), or more if desired (see Tips)

2 sprigs fresh thyme or 1/2 teaspoon dried thyme, or more if needed

1 cup pasta sauce

Two 10-ounce packages frozen artichoke hearts (rinse away any ice crystals), or two 8.5-ounce cans, drained (see Tips)

Salt and freshly ground pepper to taste

2 tablespoons minced fresh parsley, for garnish

Heat 1 tablespoon of oil in the cooker over medium-high heat. Brown the veal in 4 batches, 4 to 6 minutes per batch, adding extra oil as needed. Set the browned veal aside.

Add the wine and leeks. Stir well to scrape up any browned bits stuck to the bottom of the cooker. Cook over medium-high heat until most of the wine has evaporated, about 2 minutes. Add the broth, celery, olives, thyme, reserved veal with accumulated juices, and frozen artichoke hearts. (It's OK if they're frozen into a block.) Pour the pasta sauce on top. *Do not stir.*

Lock the lid in place. Over high heat, bring to high pressure. Reduce the heat just enough to maintain high pressure and cook for 12 minutes. Quick-release the pressure. Remove the lid, tilting it away from you to allow excess steam to escape.

If you wish, add more olives plus additional thyme, salt, and pepper. If using canned artichoke hearts, add them at this time and cook just until heated. Garnish individual portions with parsley.

SERVES 4

TIPS

Small olives are a good choice since they can easily be distributed throughout the dish. (Warn guests if you haven't pitted them.) Cut large olives in half. Since olives can be quite salty, add a conservative amount at the beginning and more at the end, if you wish.

Opt for frozen artichoke hearts, if available, as they have better flavor and texture. If using canned, halve them, if you wish. Add them at the end and cook only until thoroughly heated, 1 to 2 minutes.

CATALAN VEAL STEW

I love the bold flavors of the Spanish kitchen, so a pressure-cooked rendition of this saffron-infused stew began simmering in my mind as soon as I spotted the recipe in Penelope Casas' The Foods & Wines of Spain. The rich tomato-flecked sauce, chunky with mushrooms, looks and tastes best when served over white rice.

12 MINUTES HIGH PRESSURE

5 MINUTES ADDITIONAL COOKING

Generous 1/2 teaspoon loosely packed saffron threads

1 tablespoon warm water

2 1/2 pounds boneless veal shoulder, cut into 1 1/2-inch cubes, well trimmed

2 tablespoons all-purpose flour

2 to 3 tablespoons olive oil

1 cup veal or chicken broth

1 cup coarsely chopped red onions

1 large bay leaf

6 large fresh or canned plum tomatoes, halved lengthwise

1/2 teaspoon salt, or to taste

1/2 teaspoon dried thyme leaves

1 clove garlic, pushed through a press

1/2 pound cremini or button mushrooms, halved and sliced

2 to 3 teaspoons sherry wine or balsamic vinegar (optional)

Crumble the saffron into a small bowl and stir in the water. Set aside.

Lightly dust the veal on both sides with flour. Heat 1 tablespoon of oil over medium-high heat and brown the veal in 4 batches, 4 to 6 minutes per batch, adding extra oil as needed. Transfer the browned veal to a platter.

Add the broth and stir well, taking care to scrape up any browned bits stuck to the bottom of the cooker. Add the onions, browned veal with accumulated juices, and bay leaf. Set the tomatoes on top and sprinkle with salt. *Do not stir.*

Lock the lid in place. Over high heat, bring to high pressure. Lower the heat to maintain high pressure and cook for 12 minutes. Quick-release the pressure.

Remove the lid, tilting it away from you to allow any excess steam to escape. If the veal is not sufficiently tender, return to high pressure for 5 minutes more.

Remove the bay leaf and stir in the saffron with its steeping water, the thyme, garlic, and mushrooms. Simmer uncovered over medium heat, stirring occasionally, until the garlic loses its raw edge and the mushrooms are tender, about 5 minutes. Adjust the seasonings, adding more salt and a bit of vinegar, if needed, to bring out the flavors. Serve in large, deep plates over rice.

SERVES 4

VEAL SHANKS WITH PORCINI, WHITE BEANS, AND ESCAROLE

Here is an elegant dish to serve company: veal shanks on a bed of meltingly soft beans cooked in porcini broth that is brightened by patches of wilted escarole. The last-minute addition of lemon zest gives the dish a lively finish.

When shopping for veal shanks (also called shins, and often referred to by their Italian name, osso buco), you'll find that they are cut into circular pieces with the marrow bone in the middle. Look for shanks approximately 2 inches thick that weigh about 10 ounces each, but don't be concerned if the shanks vary by an ounce or two. If the butcher has tied the shanks with string, leave it in place to help the meat hold its shape. The bone inevitably falls out during cooking; just pop it back in place before serving.

Shanks are so flavorful that it's not necessary to brown them first. Nor is it necessary to presoak the beans, which should be just about done by the time the veal is tender.

30 MINUTES HIGH PRESSURE PLUS 10-MINUTE NATURAL PRESSURE RELEASE (SHANKS)

6 MINUTES ADDITIONAL COOKING

¾ ounce (about ¾ cup) dried porcini mushrooms

2 cups boiling water

1 tablespoon olive oil

2 cups thinly sliced leeks or coarsely chopped onions

½ cup dry white wine or vermouth

2½ cups chicken or veal broth, preferably unsalted (see Tip)

2 teaspoons dried rosemary leaves, broken into bits

1 cup cannellini, navy, or Great Northern beans, picked over and rinsed

4 veal shanks, about 10 ounces each

3 tablespoons tomato paste

1 to 2 cloves garlic, pushed through a press

Salt and freshly ground black pepper to taste

1 pound escarole, chopped

½ teaspoon lemon zest, or more to taste

Set the porcini in a bowl and pour the boiling water on top. Cover and let steep until the mushrooms are soft, about 10 minutes. Lift the porcini out with a slotted spoon and coarsely chop if necessary. Set the porcini and mushroom broth aside.

Over medium-high heat, heat the oil in the cooker. Cook the leeks, stirring frequently, until they begin to soften, about 3 minutes. Add the wine and cook over high heat until the wine is reduced by half, about 1 minute.

Add the broth, rosemary, beans, and porcini. Add the reserved mushroom broth, pouring the broth out gently so that any sediment remains on the bottom of the bowl. Add the shanks.

Lock the lid in place. Over high heat, bring to high pressure. Lower the heat to maintain high pressure and cook for 30 minutes. Let the pressure drop naturally for 10 minutes. Quick-release any remaining pressure. Remove the lid, tilting it away from you to allow any excess steam to escape.

Carefully remove the shanks and set aside. (They may be falling off the bone.) Taste the beans and, if they are not sufficiently tender, return to high pressure for 5 minutes more.

Stir in the tomato paste, garlic, and salt and pepper. Over high heat, bring to a boil. Stir in the escarole, submerging it in the liquid with the back of a spoon. Set (but do not lock) the lid in place and cook over medium heat until the escarole is tender, about 6 minutes.

Just before serving, add lemon zest to taste and adjust the seasonings. Return the shanks to the cooker to heat throughout.

To serve, divide the beans, escarole, and broth among 4 large soup bowls. Place a shank in the center on top, with the marrow bone in place.

SERVES 4

TIP

If using canned broth, be sure it is reduced-sodium; use 1½ cups broth and 1 cup water. Too much salt at the early stage of cooking will prevent the beans from tenderizing properly.

FISH AND SEAFOOD

SEAFOOD UNDER PRESSURE

I love seafood and I love the pressure cooker, but I don't recommend cooking fish or other seafood under pressure: It's just too delicate, and the risk of over-cooking is too great. Besides, seafood cooks very quickly by standard techniques.

So why this chapter? It does make practical sense to pressure-cook the potatoes for a seafood chowder or the risotto that will be dotted with shrimp, thereby reducing the cooking time of such dishes to about 5 minutes.

This is a short section but one that reveals how the pressure cooker can play a vital role in speeding up the creation of hearty seafood one-pots.

ASTURIAN BEANS AND CLAMS

While leafing through Penelope Casas' definitive The Foods & Wines of Spain, *I was irresistibly drawn to this lusty seafood dish prepared in the northern region of Asturias. I'd never experienced the combination of beans and clams before making this dish, but concluded after my first taste that they are memorable partners.*

In this pressure-cooker version, I've followed Penelope's recipe quite loosely and added some collards for an extra boost of flavor and nutrition. First, the clams are steamed open in 2 batches and set aside. If you wish to save time, steam half of the clams in another pot alongside the cooker—or try the mussel variation.

After cooking the beans under pressure, stir in the opened clams for a quick reheating before serving. Allow 5 to 6 clams per person; a few clams may not open and will have to be discarded. You're likely to have a portion or two of beans left over for lunch the next day. Delicious over rice. Lucky you.

12 MINUTES HIGH PRESSURE

3 TO 5 MINUTES ADDITIONAL COOKING

2 cups cannellini or Great Northern beans, picked over and rinsed, soaked overnight in ample water to cover or speed-soaked (page 24)

3 cups water, or more as needed

2 dozen littleneck clams, scrubbed to remove sand

1 tablespoon olive oil

2 cups coarsely chopped onions

2 cups fish broth or 16 ounces bottled clam juice

1 tablespoon sweet paprika

¼ teaspoon crushed red pepper flakes, or more to taste

½ pound collard greens or kale, trimmed, stems thinly sliced and leaves coarsely chopped

½ teaspoon crumbled saffron threads steeped in 2 tablespoons warm water

¾ teaspoon salt, or to taste

2 large cloves garlic, pushed through a press

1 large red bell pepper, roasted (page 241), seeded, and diced

¼ cup chopped fresh parsley, for garnish

continued

Drain and rinse the beans. Set aside.

Bring the water to a boil in the cooker. Set 1 dozen clams in the water and set (but do not lock) the lid in place. Cook over high heat, shaking the cooker vigorously from side to side frequently, until one or more of the clams pop open. (You will probably hear a knocking against the sides of the cooker.) Start checking after 3 minutes and every minute or so thereafter, removing clams as they open and setting them in a large bowl. Continue until all or most of the clams have opened, which can take as long as 12 minutes. Discard any clams that do not open. Repeat with the remaining dozen clams, adding water to the cooker if necessary. Pour the clam-steaming liquid through a fine-meshed strainer into a measuring cup. (Take care to leave behind any sandy residue in the bottom of the cooker.) Add water to the clam liquid, if needed, to equal a total of 2 cups.

Rinse and thoroughly dry the cooker. Heat the oil in the cooker over medium-high heat. Cook the onions, stirring frequently, for 1 minute. Add the clam-steaming liquid, fish broth, paprika, red pepper flakes, reserved beans, and collards.

Lock the lid in place. Over high heat, bring to high pressure. Lower the heat just enough to maintain high pressure and cook for 12 minutes. Reduce pressure with a quick-release method. Remove the lid, tilting it away from you to allow any excess steam to escape.

Taste the beans. If they are not sufficiently tender, return to high pressure for 2 to 3 minutes more, or cook at a gentle boil, covered, until done. When the beans are done, add the saffron with its steeping liquid, the salt, garlic, and more crushed red pepper flakes, if needed. Cook over medium heat until the flavors "bloom" and the garlic loses its raw edge, 3 to 5 minutes. (The mixture may be slightly soupy, which is fine.)

Just before serving, stir in the roasted red pepper and clams, plus any liquid they have released. Cover and cook over medium heat just until the clams are hot, about 30 seconds. (Take care not to overcook the clams as they will get tough.) Ladle the beans and clams into large, shallow soup bowls, allowing 5 or 6 clams per portion. Sprinkle each portion lightly with parsley.

SERVES 4

ASTURIAN BEANS WITH MUSSELS

Omit the clams and substitute 2 pounds scrubbed, debearded mussels. Steam open in 2 batches following the instructions for clams; however, it will take only about 3 minutes for the mussels to open. Proceed as directed.

SCROD AND CORN CHOWDER

With its bright flecks of corn and red pepper set against a milky white back-drop, this is a pretty chowder. It's a good choice when you're in the mood for a delicate and soothing entrée. No unexpected taste sensations: just plain good.

Make it as rich or lean as you like, depending upon your choice of cream or milk and your generosity with the butter.

3 MINUTES HIGH PRESSURE

2 TO 3 MINUTES ADDITIONAL COOKING

1 tablespoon butter

1 1/2 cups coarsely chopped onions

16 ounces bottled clam juice

1 cup fish broth or water

1 pound red-skinned or Yukon Gold potatoes, peeled and cut into
  1/2-inch dice

3 medium ribs celery, halved lengthwise and cut into 1/4-inch slices

1 small red bell pepper, seeded and diced

1/2 teaspoon dried thyme leaves, or more to taste

3/4 teaspoon salt, or to taste

1 1/2 pounds scrod fillets, cut into 1-inch chunks

2 cups fresh or frozen corn (rinse away any ice crystals)

1/2 cup heavy cream or milk

Freshly ground white or black pepper to taste

2 tablespoons minced fresh parsley or snipped chives, for garnish

4 thin pats butter, for garnish (optional)

Heat the butter in the cooker over medium-high heat until it begins to foam. Cook the onions, stirring frequently, until they begin to soften, about 2 minutes. Add the clam juice, broth, potatoes, celery, red bell pepper, thyme, and salt.

Lock the lid in place. Over high heat, bring to high pressure. Lower the heat just enough to maintain high pressure and cook for 3 minutes. Quick-release the pressure. Remove the lid, tilting it away from you to allow any excess steam to escape.

Return the mixture to a gentle boil over medium heat. Add more thyme, if needed. Add the scrod and corn. Cover and cook just until the scrod becomes opaque and easily flakes, 2 to 3 minutes. Gently stir in the cream and salt and pepper to taste. Garnish each portion with parsley and a pat of butter, if you wish.

SERVES 4

SALMON AND CORN CHOWDER

Substitute skinned salmon fillets for all or part of the scrod.

FISH STEW WITH SWISS CHARD

*This simple fish stew is made in two steps. First, you pressure-cook the pota-
toes with fish broth, tomatoes, and Swiss chard stems. Then you add some
perky green chard leaves and chunks of fish and cook them in the standard
way. A hint of orange zest added at the end gives the stew a memorable finish.*

3 MINUTES HIGH PRESSURE

6 TO 10 MINUTES ADDITIONAL COOKING

1 pound Swiss chard

1 tablespoon olive oil

1 cup thinly sliced leeks or coarsely chopped onions

1 teaspoon whole fennel seeds

2 cups fish broth or 16 ounces bottled clam juice

One 15-ounce can diced tomatoes, with liquid

1 pound Yukon Gold or red-skinned potatoes, trimmed and cut into
  ½-inch dice (see Tip)

Salt and freshly ground pepper to taste

1 small clove garlic, pushed through a press

1½ pounds firm-fleshed white fish fillets, such as hake, scrod, haddock,
  monkfish, or white snapper, cut into 1-inch chunks

1 teaspoon grated orange zest

Holding the chard in a bunch, trim off and discard the bottom half inch or so of
stems. Working with one leaf at a time, gently rip each green leaf from the stem
and midrib, discarding any bruised leaves or stems as you go. Cut the stems and
midribs into ½-inch slices. Rinse thoroughly, drain, and set aside. Chop the
leaves coarsely or tear them. Rinse and set aside separately.

Heat the oil in the cooker over medium-high heat. Cook the leeks and fennel
seeds, stirring frequently, for 1 minute. Add the fish broth, tomatoes, chard
stems, and potatoes.

Lock the lid in place. Over high heat, bring to high pressure. Reduce the heat just
enough to maintain high pressure and cook for 3 minutes. Quick-release the pressure. Remove the lid, tilting it away from you to allow excess steam to escape.

Set the cooker over medium heat. Add the salt, pepper, and garlic. Push the potatoes aside and add the chard leaves, stirring them into the hot mixture until they wilt. Cook for 3 minutes, stirring occasionally. Push the potatoes and chard aside and submerge the fish chunks as much as possible in the liquid. Cook over medium heat at a gentle boil, stirring occasionally, until the fish becomes opaque and easily flakes, 3 to 7 minutes depending upon the type of fish. Stir in the orange zest and serve immediately.

SERVES 4

TIP

It's not necessary to peel the potatoes. Most of the skins fall off and disappear into the stew.

SHRIMP RISOTTO WITH CAPERS AND ANCHOVIES

To make this risotto, quickly sauté the shrimp with lots of garlic and set them aside. (If you've peeled the shrimp yourself, you can prepare a fine broth from the shells; see page 23.)

Then cook the rice under pressure and, when it's done, season it with a savory mixture of anchovies, capers, parsley, and other ingredients traditionally used to prepare an Italian salsa verde. The anchovies dissolve, bringing a bolder taste of the sea to the otherwise delicate shrimp, which are stirred in at the very end.

Although Italian cooks avoid the use of Parmesan with fish and seafood, I sometimes sprinkle a bit on top of this risotto. You probably won't need any added salt (and be sure to use unsalted broth) since the anchovies are so salty.

4 MINUTES HIGH PRESSURE

2 TO 4 MINUTES ADDITIONAL COOKING

SALSA VERDE
¾ cup tightly packed fresh flat-leaf parsley (leaves only)
¼ cup drained capers
8 anchovy fillets (oil-packed)
1 teaspoon grated lemon zest
3 tablespoons freshly squeezed lemon juice

RISOTTO
2 tablespoons olive oil
1 tablespoon butter
1¼ pounds shrimp, shelled, deveined, and cut into 1-inch pieces
1 tablespoon minced garlic
½ cup minced shallots or onions
2 cups arborio rice
¾ cup dry red or white wine
5½ cups unsalted shrimp, fish, or vegetable broth
Freshly ground black pepper to taste
¼ cup minced fresh parsley, for garnish

Place the ingredients for the Salsa Verde in the bowl of a food processor and pulse a few times to chop. Scrape down the bowl and pulse a few times again to create a coarse mash. Set aside.

For the risotto, heat 1 tablespoon of the oil and the butter in the cooker over medium-high heat until they begin to sizzle. Add the shrimp and garlic and cook, stirring almost constantly, scraping up any garlic that sticks to the bottom of the cooker, until the shrimp turns bright pink on all sides, 1½ to 2 minutes. Transfer the shrimp and garlic to a bowl and set aside.

Heat the remaining tablespoon of oil in the cooker. Over medium-high heat, cook the shallots for 1 minute, stirring constantly. Add the rice and stir to coat with the oil. Add the wine and take care to scrape up any browned bits stuck to the bottom of the cooker. Continue cooking over medium-high heat until most of the wine has evaporated, about 30 seconds. Add the broth and a few twists of black pepper.

Lock the lid in place. Over high heat, bring to high pressure. Lower the heat to just enough to maintain high pressure and cook for 4 minutes. Quick-release the pressure by setting the cooker under cold running water. Remove the lid, tilting it away from you to allow any excess steam to escape.

Stir in the Salsa Verde and boil over medium-high heat, stirring constantly, until the rice is tender but still a bit chewy and the risotto loses most of its soupiness and becomes creamy and thick, 2 to 4 minutes. Stir in the shrimp and cook just until hot, about 20 seconds. Serve immediately, garnished with parsley.

SERVES 4

SOUTH AMERICAN
SEAFOOD STEW

The cooking of the late chef Felipe Rojas-Lombardy has always been an inspiration to me. At his Manhattan restaurant and cabaret, The Ballroom, Felipe enticed guests with piquant food that imaginatively interpreted the ingredients of his native Peru. Fortunately, Felipe has left his culinary legacy in two fine cookbooks, Soup, Beautiful Soup *and* The Art of South American Cooking.

I have combined some of Felipe's ideas to create this unusual dish. The recipe calls for numerous South American vegetables, readily available in Hispanic groceries. (Check the Guide to Ingredients, page 233, for details.) If you have trouble finding them, I've suggested common alternatives that work perfectly well.

If you use annatto oil, the dish develops an appealing brownish-red color and a haunting earthy flavor. Annatto seeds (often labeled achiote*) are available in the Hispanic section of most supermarkets and by mail order from spice merchants.*

3 MINUTES HIGH PRESSURE

3 TO 4 MINUTES ADDITIONAL COOKING

1½ tablespoons annatto oil (page 233) or 1½ tablespoons olive oil plus
   ½ teaspoon sweet paprika

1 cup coarsely chopped onions

2 teaspoons whole cumin seeds

3 cups fish broth or 24 ounces bottled clam juice

¼ teaspoon crushed red pepper flakes

2 large bay leaves

1¼ pounds yellow plantains or Yukon Gold potatoes, peeled and cut
   into ½-inch pieces

1½ pounds calabaza pumpkin or butternut squash, peeled and cut into
   1½-inch chunks

One 15-ounce can diced tomatoes or whole plum tomatoes, chopped,
   with liquid

1 teaspoon salt, or to taste

1 to 2 cloves garlic, pushed through a press

1 teaspoon dried oregano leaves

1 pound firm-fleshed white fish fillets, such as striped bass, flounder, or scrod, cut into 1-inch chunks

½ pound small or medium shrimp, shelled and deveined

¼ cup chopped fresh cilantro

2 tablespoons freshly squeezed lime juice, or more to taste

Heat the oil in the cooker over medium-high heat. Cook the onions and cumin, stirring frequently, for 2 minutes. Add the fish broth, red pepper flakes, bay leaves, and plantains. Set the calabaza on top. Pour the tomatoes over the squash and sprinkle with salt. *Do not stir.*

Lock the lid in place. Over high heat, bring to high pressure. Reduce the heat just enough to maintain high pressure and cook for 3 minutes. Quick-release the pressure. Remove the lid, tilting it away from you to allow excess steam to escape.

Stir well as you add the garlic and oregano; remove the bay leaves. (Most of the calabaza is likely to melt into a puree and thicken the sauce.) Over medium heat, bring to a gentle boil. Add the fish and cook, uncovered, for 2 minutes, stirring gently once or twice. Add the shrimp and cook until the fish becomes opaque and easily flakes and the shrimp turns pink, 1 to 2 minutes more.

Adjust for salt and stir in the cilantro and enough lime juice to sharpen the flavors and give the stew a slight acid edge. Serve in large soup bowls.

SERVES 5 TO 6

BEANS

BEANS UNDER PRESSURE

Although beans show up here and there throughout the book, in this chapter they stand in the limelight. I sometimes think of beans as the chicken of the vegetable kingdom. Because of their easy-going flavor and texture, beans are extremely versatile and go well with a wide array of seasonings and other ingredients. Sometimes I'll suggest a particular bean because of its shape, color, or cooking time; other times I'll select the bean that has traditionally been used to prepare a particular dish.

I'm crazy about beans in all of their shapes, colors, and sizes. If you think they're heavy or dull, I hope you'll allow the recipes that follow to change your perception. To review the basics of pressure-cooking beans, consult pages 24 to 27.

WHITE BEAN SOUP WITH PORTOBELLOS, ESCAROLE, AND PARSLEY PESTO

This hearty Italian soup gets an elegant touch with the addition of chopped portobello mushrooms that are quickly cooked and then set aside until the beans are done. You can use one type of white bean—such as cannellini, Great Northern, or navy—or a mixture.

Just before serving, give the soup a lively punch of color and flavor with a generous dollop of parsley pesto.

12 MINUTES HIGH PRESSURE

1 TO 2 MINUTES ADDITIONAL COOKING

2 cups white beans, picked over and rinsed, soaked overnight in ample water to cover or speed-soaked (page 24)

1¼ pounds portobellos, cremini, or large button mushrooms

2 tablespoons olive oil

1 medium red bell pepper, seeded and diced

1 tablespoon minced garlic

6 cups chicken or vegetable broth

1½ cups thinly sliced leeks or coarsely chopped onions

5 tablespoons tomato paste

⅓ cup dry red wine or vermouth

2½ teaspoons Italian herb blend (page 238 or store-bought)

2 large bay leaves

1½ pounds escarole, trimmed and coarsely chopped

Salt and freshly ground black pepper to taste

Parsley Pesto (recipe follows)

Freshly grated Parmesan or Pecorino Romano cheese (optional)

Drain and rinse the beans. Set aside.

Trim the mushrooms. If the portobellos have stems, chop them and set aside. Slice the caps into ¾-inch pieces. If using cremini or button mushrooms, cut the mushrooms in half or quarters to approximately equal ¾-inch chunks.

continued

Heat 1½ tablespoons of oil in the cooker over medium-high heat. Add the mushrooms (excluding stems), red bell pepper, and garlic and stir to coat the vegetables with oil. Add ½ cup of the broth and cook over medium heat at a gentle boil, stirring occasionally, until the mushrooms are tender, 3 to 4 minutes. Transfer the cooked vegetables and any remaining broth to a bowl and set aside.

Wipe the cooker dry with a paper towel and heat the remaining ½ tablespoon of oil over medium-high heat. Cook the leeks and 2 tablespoons of the tomato paste, stirring frequently, until the leeks are slightly softened, about 3 minutes. Add the red wine and cook over high heat, scraping up any browned bits sticking to the bottom of the cooker. Cook until most of the wine evaporates, about 1 minute. Add the remaining broth, beans, chopped portobello stems (if you have any), herbs, and bay leaves. Pile the escarole on top. (Don't be concerned if the cooker is full beyond the maximum recommended capacity; the greens will shrink dramatically as the soup comes up to pressure.)

Lock the lid in place. Over high heat, bring to high pressure. (This may take about 5 minutes.) Lower the heat just enough to maintain high pressure and cook for 12 minutes. Quick-release the pressure by setting the cooker under cold running water. Remove the lid, tilting it away from you to allow excess steam to escape.

Blend in the remaining 3 tablespoons of tomato paste by mashing it against the side of the cooker with a fork and stirring. Remove the bay leaves, and add salt and pepper. Stir in the reserved mushrooms and red pepper and continue cooking just until thoroughly heated. Serve each portion of soup with a heaping tablespoon of parsley pesto set in the center. Pass any extra pesto and some grated cheese, if you wish, on the side.

SERVES 6

PARSLEY PESTO

1 small clove garlic, peeled (optional)

2 cups tightly packed flat-leaf parsley leaves and thin stems (from 1 very large bunch)

Generous ½ cup walnuts

½ cup freshly grated Parmesan or Pecorino Romano cheese, plus more to pass at the table

½ teaspoon salt, or to taste

2 tablespoons olive oil

1 to 2 tablespoons water (optional)

If using the garlic, pop it through the feed tube of a food processor with the motor running. Scrape down the work bowl, add the parsley and walnuts, and process until finely chopped. Scrape down the bowl, and add the cheese and salt. With the motor running, pour the olive oil into the feed tube and process to create a thick (but not stiff) paste, adding water if needed. Adjust for salt and set aside until needed. Refrigerate any leftovers in a tightly sealed container for up to 3 days.

MAKES ABOUT 1 CUP

SPLIT PEA-VEGETABLE SOUP WITH MINT CREAM

Fragrant with the spices of North Africa, the split peas in this soup dissolve into a puree that becomes a backdrop for chunks of carrots, squash, and parsnips. Each spoonful offers flavor bursts of caraway, cumin, and hot pepper, and a mint-flecked sour cream topping provides a cooling contrast.

The split peas are given a head start and then the vegetables are added for a final 3 minutes. You can streamline your prep time by chopping the vegetables and making the mint cream while the split peas are cooking. It's actually a good idea to let the mint cream sit for a few minutes before serving to give the flavors time to meld.

The soup thickens considerably upon standing or refrigeration. When you reheat it, thin to desired consistency by blending in additional broth or water.

12 MINUTES HIGH PRESSURE

1 tablespoon olive oil

1 1/2 cups coarsely chopped onions

1 1/2 teaspoons whole cumin seeds, or more to taste

1 teaspoon caraway seeds, or more to taste

1/4 teaspoon crushed red pepper flakes, or more to taste

5 cups chicken or vegetable broth, or more if needed

1 cup green split peas, picked over and rinsed

1 teaspoon salt, or to taste

4 medium carrots, peeled and cut into 3/4-inch slices

1 1/2 pounds butternut squash, peeled, seeded, and cut into 1-inch chunks

3/4 pound parsnips or Yukon Gold potatoes, peeled and cut into 1-inch chunks

MINT CREAM

1/2 cup sour cream or yogurt

3 tablespoons finely chopped fresh mint or 2 teaspoons dried mint leaves, or more to taste

1 teaspoon ground coriander seeds, or more to taste

Salt to taste

Heat the oil in the cooker over medium-high heat. Cook the onions, cumin, caraway, and red pepper flakes, stirring frequently, for 1 minute. Add the broth and split peas.

Lock the lid in place. Over high heat, bring to high pressure. Reduce the heat just enough to maintain high pressure and cook for 9 minutes. While the soup is cooking, prepare the Mint Cream in a small bowl by blending the sour cream, mint (if using dried mint, rub it between your fingers to crush and release the flavor), coriander, and salt to taste. Set aside.

When the timer rings, quick-release the pressure by placing the cooker under cold running water. Remove the lid, tilting it away from you to allow excess steam to escape.

Stir well, taking care to integrate any split peas that are sticking to the bottom of the cooker. If the mixture is too thick, thin it to a soupy consistency with additional broth or water. Season with salt and additional spices, if needed. Add the carrots, squash, and parsnips.

Lock the lid in place and, over high heat, return to high pressure. Reduce the heat just enough to maintain high pressure and cook for another 3 minutes. Quick-release the pressure by placing the cooker under cold running water. Remove the lid, tilting it away from you to allow excess steam to escape. If the vegetables are not quite tender, set (but do not lock) the lid in place and cook over medium heat until done.

Stir the soup well. Add more salt, if needed. Taste the Mint Cream and adjust the seasonings. Serve the soup in large bowls, with a generous dollop of Mint Cream in the middle of each portion. Pass any remaining Mint Cream in a small bowl at the table.

SERVES 4

LENTIL TABOULI SOUP

This recipe includes all of the ingredients contained in a great tabouli: bulgur wheat, tomatoes, lemon juice, and lots of parsley. (You'll need two good-sized bunches. Opt for the flat-leaf variety if it's available.) I've put a new slant on the dish by combining all of these ingredients in a lentil soup.

Since the acid in the lemon juice quickly dulls parsley's bright color, you might like to add lemon juice only to the portion you are planning to serve. Leftovers are likely to need some extra lemon juice anyway.

Coarse bulgur is available in most health-food stores and in supermarkets under the Goya label.

10 MINUTES HIGH PRESSURE

2 MINUTES ADDITIONAL COOKING

2 tablespoons olive oil

2 cups coarsely chopped onions

6 cups vegetable broth

1 1/2 cups brown lentils

1/3 cup coarse bulgur

1/4 teaspoon crushed red pepper flakes (optional)

1 to 2 cloves garlic, pushed through a press

3 cups seeded and finely diced plum tomatoes

1 tablespoon finely chopped fresh mint or 1 1/2 teaspoons dried mint, or more to taste

1 1/4 teaspoons salt, or to taste

1 cup loosely packed minced fresh parsley, or more to taste

1 to 3 tablespoons freshly squeezed lemon juice

Over medium-high heat, heat 1 tablespoon of the oil in the cooker. Cook the onions, stirring frequently, for 2 minutes. Add the broth and stir well to scrape up any browned bits sticking to the bottom of the cooker. Add the lentils, bulgur, and red pepper flakes, if using.

Lock the lid in place. Over high heat, bring to high pressure. Lower the heat just enough to maintain high pressure and cook for 10 minutes. Quick-release the pressure. Remove the lid, tilting it away from you to allow any excess steam to escape.

Stir in the garlic, tomatoes, the remaining tablespoon of olive oil, mint, and salt. Simmer until the garlic loses its raw taste, about 2 minutes. Blend in the parsley and lemon juice. Taste and add more mint, parsley, and lemon juice, if you wish. (I like the soup very lemony and use about 3 tablespoons for the potful, but this is a matter of taste.) Serve in large soup bowls.

SERVES 4 TO 6

BLACK BEAN CHILI WITH SQUASH AND CORN

The fine flavor and creamy texture of black beans produce a memorable chili. But eating the beans on their own can be a bit monotonous. So after they are almost cooked, I stir in brightly colored diced tomatoes, squash, and corn for welcome splashes of color.

If you enjoy the yeasty taste and slight bitter edge of beer, use it for part of the cooking liquid. (If you don't eat the chili right away, the faint bitterness fades in an hour or two.) Otherwise, use broth.

This starts out a fairly thick chili and thickens even more upon standing. If you wish, thin it with additional broth or water.

12 MINUTES UNDER PRESSURE

3 MINUTES ADDITIONAL COOKING

2 1/2 cups (1 pound) dried black beans, picked over and rinsed, soaked overnight in ample water to cover, or speed-soaked (page 24)

1 tablespoon olive oil

2 teaspoons whole cumin seeds

2 cups coarsely chopped onions

1 1/2 cups chicken, turkey, or vegetable broth

1 1/2 cups (12-ounce bottle) lager beer or additional broth

1 1/2 tablespoons mild chili powder, or more to taste

2 teaspoons fennel seeds

1/2 teaspoon ground cinnamon

1 1/2 teaspoons salt, or to taste

2 pounds butternut squash, peeled, seeded, and cut into 1-inch cubes (see Tip)

2 teaspoons dried oregano leaves

2 cloves garlic, pushed through a press

One 15-ounce can diced tomatoes with green chiles, with liquid, or 2 cups finely chopped fresh tomatoes plus 1 to 2 jalapeños, seeded and finely chopped

1 1/2 cups fresh or frozen corn (rinse away any ice crystals)

2 large red bell peppers, roasted (page 241), seeded and cut into 1/2-inch squares (optional)

¼ cup chopped fresh cilantro, or more to taste

Tabasco sauce to taste

1 cup Cilantro-Lime Cream (page 43) or plain sour cream, for garnish

Drain and rinse the beans. Set aside.

Heat the oil in the cooker over medium-high heat. Add the cumin and onions and cook, stirring frequently, for 1 minute. Add the broth, beer (or additional broth), reserved beans, chili powder, fennel, and cinnamon.

Lock the lid in place. Over high heat, bring to high pressure. Lower the heat just enough to maintain high pressure and cook for 9 minutes. Quick-release the pressure. Remove the lid, tilting it away from you to allow any excess steam to escape. If the beans are not close to tender, either lock the lid in place and return to high pressure for a few minutes more, or simmer them, covered, over medium heat until just about done.

Stir in the salt, squash, oregano, and additional chili powder, if you think it's needed. Over high heat, return to high pressure. Lower the heat just enough to maintain high pressure and cook for 3 minutes. Quick-release the pressure. Remove the lid, tilting it away from you to allow excess steam to escape.

Add the garlic, tomatoes, corn, and roasted red peppers, if using, and simmer over medium heat until the squash is tender and the garlic loses its raw edge, about 3 minutes.

Just before serving, stir in the cilantro and Tabasco sauce to taste. Serve in large, shallow bowls with a generous dollop of Cilantro-Lime Cream on top. Pass extra Cilantro-Lime Cream in a bowl.

SERVES 7 TO 8

TIP

If you can find kabocha or delicata squash, by all means use these instead. (They are frequently sold in farmers' markets and health-food stores that carry organic produce.) You are sure to enjoy the intense flavor of these squash and the fact that you don't have to scrape off their pretty peels.

PINTO, ZUCCHINI, AND CRACKED HOMINY CHILI

Hominy—with its faint corn flavor and pleasantly chewy texture—deserves to be known far beyond the borders of Arizona and New Mexico. I was therefore pleased to discover that Goya is now distributing dried, cracked hominy (also called posole) *to supermarkets nationwide. If you can find only canned hominy, try the variation below.*

Cracked hominy cooks up real well with pintos and chili powder, no great surprise since these ingredients are all big players in the southwestern kitchen. For best success, use a good-quality blend of mild chili powder and add heat to taste with Tabasco.

10 MINUTES HIGH PRESSURE

6 TO 8 MINUTES ADDITIONAL COOKING

1 cup dried pinto beans, picked over and rinsed, soaked overnight in ample water to cover, or speed-soaked (page 24)

1 cup dried, cracked hominy (Goya's white hominy corn), rinsed, then soaked together with the pintos

1 tablespoon olive oil

2 cups coarsely chopped onions

1 ½ tablespoons minced garlic

1 ½ teaspoons whole cumin seeds

2 cups chicken or turkey broth, or water

2 tablespoons mild chili powder, or more to taste

2 large bay leaves

1 large green bell pepper, seeded and diced

One 15-ounce can diced tomatoes with green chiles, with liquid, or 2 cups chopped plum tomatoes plus 1 to 2 jalapeños, seeded and diced

1 teaspoon salt, or to taste

1 teaspoon dried oregano leaves

3 medium zucchini or yellow squash, quartered lengthwise and cut into ½-inch pieces

¼ cup chopped fresh cilantro, or more to taste

Freshly ground black pepper to taste

Tabasco sauce to taste

1 cup grated sharp cheddar cheese, preferably smoked

Drain and rinse the beans and hominy. Set aside.

Over medium-high heat, heat the oil in the cooker. Cook the onions, stirring frequently, until slightly softened, about 3 minutes. Reduce the heat to medium and stir in the garlic and cumin. Cook until the onions begin to brown, an additional minute or two. Transfer the onion mixture to a small bowl and set aside.

Add the broth and take care to scrape up any browned bits from the bottom of the cooker. Add the chili powder, bay leaves, reserved beans and hominy, and green pepper.

Lock the lid in place. Over high heat, bring to high pressure. Reduce the heat just enough to maintain high pressure and cook for 10 minutes. Quick-release the pressure. Remove the lid, tilting it away from you to allow excess steam to escape. If the beans or hominy (which should be soft but a bit chewy) are not close to tender, set (but do not lock) the lid in place and cook over medium heat, stirring occasionally, until just about done.

Stir well. Remove the bay leaves. Add the reserved onion mixture, diced tomatoes, salt, and additional chili powder, if needed. Bring to a boil. Stir in the oregano and zucchini. Set (but do not lock) the lid in place and cook over medium heat, stirring occasionally, until the zucchini are tender-crisp, 6 to 8 minutes.

Stir in the cilantro. Adjust the seasonings and add black pepper and Tabasco. Ladle into large bowls. Sprinkle each portion with a heaping tablespoon of grated cheese and pass the remaining cheese in a small bowl at the table.

SERVES 4 TO 6

PINTO, ZUCCHINI, AND CRACKED HOMINY CHILI WITH SMOKED HAM

Add 1 to 2 cups diced smoked ham or pork butt when you add the zucchini.

PINTO CHILI WITH CANNED HOMINY AND ZUCCHINI

Omit the dried hominy and substitute one 15-ounce can white hominy (posole), drained and thoroughly rinsed to wash away excess salt. Proceed as directed. If the cooked stew is too thin, mash about a half cup of beans against the side of the cooker and stir them in to thicken.

RED LENTIL DAL WITH POTATOES AND SWISS CHARD

After 5 minutes under pressure, curried red lentils melt into a thick egg-yolk yellow puree punctuated by large chunks of potatoes and the pleasing pop of toasted mustard seeds. This soupy stew is enriched with grated coconut, and a healthy portion of chopped Swiss chard leaves wilted in at the end gives it vibrant color.

A puddle of Mango Yogurt on top of each serving adds a vital flavor component, so be sure to include it.

5 MINUTES UNDER PRESSURE

5 MINUTES ADDITIONAL COOKING

2 tablespoons brown mustard seeds

1 tablespoon peanut oil or ghee (clarified butter, page 237)

2 cups coarsely chopped onions

6 cups water or 3 cups water and 3 cups chicken broth

1 1/2 cups red lentils, picked over and rinsed

1 1/2 pounds Swiss chard, stems cut into 1-inch slices, leaves coarsely chopped, thoroughly rinsed (keep stems and leaves separate)

1 1/2 pounds Yukon Gold or red-skinned potatoes, or a mixture, cut into 1-inch chunks (peeling optional)

1/2 cup dried, grated unsweetened coconut

1 tablespoon mild curry powder, or more to taste

1/8 teaspoon cayenne, or more to taste

1 large clove garlic, pushed through a press

1 1/2 teaspoons salt, or to taste

Freshly ground black pepper to taste

Mango Yogurt (page 206), for garnish

Place the mustard seeds in the cooker. Turn the heat to high. Set (but do not lock) the lid in place. As soon as you hear the seeds begin to pop, after about 1½ minutes, turn off the heat (move to a cool burner if your stove is electric) and leave the lid in place until the popping subsides. Transfer the toasted mustard seeds to a small bowl and set aside.

Heat the oil in the cooker over medium-high heat. Cook the onions for 2 minutes, stirring frequently. Add the water, lentils (break up any large clumps that have formed after rinsing), Swiss chard stems, potatoes, coconut, curry powder, and cayenne.

Lock the lid in place. Over high heat, bring to high pressure. Lower the heat just enough to maintain high pressure and cook for 5 minutes. Quick release the pressure by setting the cooker under cold running water. Remove the lid, tilting it away from you to allow excess steam to escape.

Set the cooker over medium heat. Stir in the garlic, salt, and pepper. Add additional curry powder and cayenne, if needed. Stir in the Swiss chard leaves in 2 batches, allowing the first batch to wilt before adding the second.

Cook over medium heat at a steady boil, stirring occasionally, until the chard leaves are tender, about 5 minutes. Stir in the reserved mustard seeds. Serve in large soup bowls, garnished with a generous tablespoon of Mango Yogurt. Pass any remaining Mango Yogurt at the table.

SERVES 6

TWELVE-BEAN STEW WITH TURNIPS AND HORSERADISH CREAM

This is the kind of hearty stew I imagine my grandmother making on a cold winter's night back in Russia. While I'm sure she would have used some mighty fine turnips and carrots, I doubt she included twelve different types of beans. But today Goya, Jack Rabbit, and other companies make that easy to do with their colorful premixed packages, available in most supermarkets.

If you prefer to make your own mixture—a terrific way to use up odd amounts of beans in your pantry—don't feel obliged to use twelve different types. Just be sure to include about ⅓ cup split peas or lentils, which cook more quickly than other legumes and dissolve to thicken the stew. Also, soak 3 tablespoons of pearl barley along with your homemade bean mix to give added body. (If you're using a purchased bean mix, check the label and add the barley if the mix doesn't already contain some.)

Don't be tempted to omit the tasty Horseradish Cream—you can opt for nonfat sour cream, if you wish—as the stew looks too monochromatic without it. I love to use red horseradish, which gives the topping a lively pink tint, but you may have a preference for the purist white. (This is an aesthetic decision: The taste is not affected.)

The amount of horseradish you use will depend upon the potency of your batch and how much you enjoy its flavor.

14 MINUTES HIGH PRESSURE

2 cups packaged twelve-bean mix, or your own mixture plus 3 tablespoons pearl barley, picked over and rinsed, soaked overnight in ample water to cover, or speed-soaked (page 24)

½ ounce (½ cup loosely packed) dried mushrooms

2 cups boiling water, plus 3 cups tap water

1 tablespoon olive oil

2 cups thinly sliced leeks or coarsely chopped onions

2 teaspoons dried dillweed

2 large ribs celery, cut into ½-inch slices

1 1/2 pounds purple-topped turnips, peeled and cut into 1-inch chunks

3 medium carrots, peeled and cut into 1-inch chunks

1 1/4 teaspoons salt, or to taste

Horseradish Cream (page 50)

Drain the beans and barley and set aside. Place the mushrooms in a bowl and pour the boiling water on top. Cover and set aside until the mushrooms are soft, about 10 minutes. Remove the mushrooms with a slotted spoon and chop them if necessary. Set the mushrooms and soaking liquid aside.

Heat the oil in the cooker over medium-high heat. Cook the leeks, stirring frequently, until slightly softened, about 3 minutes. Add the 3 cups of tap water, chopped mushrooms, dillweed, celery, and reserved beans and barley. Pour the mushroom-soaking liquid into the cooker, taking care to leave any residue in the bottom of the bowl.

Lock the lid in place. Over high heat, bring to high pressure. Lower the heat to maintain high pressure and cook for 9 minutes. Quick-release the pressure by placing the cooker under cold running water. Remove the lid, tilting it away from you to allow excess steam to escape.

Add the turnips and carrots. Over high heat, return to high pressure. Lower the heat to maintain high pressure and cook for an additional 5 minutes. Quick-release the pressure by placing the cooker under cold running water. Remove the lid, tilting it away from you to allow any excess steam to escape.

Stir in the salt. If the beans or vegetables are not quite tender, set (but do not lock) the lid in place and cook over medium heat until done. Serve the soup in large bowls, with a generous tablespoon of Horseradish Cream in the middle. Pass any remaining Horseradish Cream at the table.

SERVES 5 TO 6

LENTILS WITH ORECCHIETTE AND CHICORY

This quickly made soupy stew puts lentils in the limelight. It is especially tasty when prepared with Italian green, French du Puy, or Spanish pardina lentils, all of which hold their shape better and are less peppery than our common brown variety. (Do not use red lentils in this dish as they quickly melt into a puree.)

First, the lentils are cooked under pressure with most of the chicory, then the pasta and remaining chicory are boiled in the open pot. Choose a medium-sized pasta with a concave shape—such as orecchiette (little ears) or shells—one that will provide some chewy texture and capture a few lentils in its "bowl." The texture of this dish is best when it's freshly made: As it sits, the pasta absorbs more liquid and becomes very soft.

Pecorino Romano cheese provides a vital flavor element, so don't be tempted to substitute Parmesan, which has a more subtle taste.

8 TO 10 MINUTES HIGH PRESSURE

7 TO 9 MINUTES ADDITIONAL COOKING (DEPENDING UPON TYPE OF PASTA)

1 pound chicory

1 tablespoon olive oil

1 cup coarsely chopped onions

3 cups chicken or vegetable broth

3 cups water

1½ cups lentils, picked over and rinsed

2 large ribs celery, halved lengthwise and cut into ½-inch slices

½ teaspoon salt, or to taste

½ tablespoon chopped fresh rosemary leaves, or ½ teaspoon dried, broken into bits, or 1 teaspoon dried oregano leaves

1 large clove garlic, pushed through a press

1½ cups dried orecchiette or shell pasta

½ to 1 cup boiling water (if needed)

¾ cup freshly grated Pecorino Romano

Freshly ground black pepper to taste

Holding the chicory in a bunch, trim off and discard the root end. Slice the stems as thinly as you can. Chop the leaves. Rinse and drain. Set aside about 4 loosely packed cups of chopped chicory leaves to be added with the pasta.

Over medium-high heat, heat the oil in the cooker. Cook the onions, stirring frequently, until lightly browned, 3 to 5 minutes. Add the broth and take care to scrape up any browned bits stuck to the bottom of the cooker. Add the water, lentils, celery, and all the chicory except for the reserved 4 cups.

Lock the lid in place. Over high heat, bring to high pressure. Reduce the heat just enough to maintain high pressure and cook for 8 minutes (brown lentils) or 10 minutes (remaining varieties). Quick-release the pressure under cold running water. Remove the lid, tilting it away from you to allow excess steam to escape. The lentils should be just short of tender. If they are still quite hard, return them to high pressure for 3 minutes more, or cover the cooker and cook over medium heat until just about done.

Set the cooker over medium heat, and stir in the salt, rosemary, garlic, reserved chicory, and pasta. Cook, uncovered, at a gentle boil, stirring occasionally to prevent the lentils and pasta from sticking to the bottom, until the pasta is tender but still a bit chewy. (Check the pasta package for timing.) Add boiling water during this time if the mixture becomes dry.

Turn off the heat and stir in ¼ cup of cheese and the pepper. Add more salt, if needed. Serve the stew in large bowls, and pass the remaining cheese at the table. Thin any leftovers with water or broth.

SERVES 6

VARIATION

Substitute an equal amount of escarole or kale for the chicory.

LENTILS WITH ORECCHIETTE AND BROCCOLI RABE

Omit the chicory and use 1 to 1½ pounds broccoli rabe. Thinly slice the stems and coarsely chop the leaves. Add all of the chopped broccoli rabe in 2 or 3 batches about a minute after you add the pasta. Stir well to submerge and wilt the leaves in the cooking liquid. Cook as directed above until the pasta is done.

CHICKPEAS IN EGGPLANT-TAHINI SAUCE

In this unusual dish, my starting point has been the Tunisian kitchen, where chickpeas are a staple and tabil—a spice mix of caraway and coriander seeds plus hot chile pepper—is the much loved equivalent of India's curry blend.

As the chickpeas become tender, the eggplant is cooked down to a puree that becomes the sauce. Bulgur wheat adds chewy substance and tahini (sesame seed paste) gives the stew a nutty richness. Resist any temptation to omit the Tomato-Cucumber Salad garnish, which brings lively crunch and color to the stew.

16 MINUTES HIGH PRESSURE

3 MINUTES ADDITIONAL COOKING

2 cups dried chickpeas, picked over and rinsed, soaked overnight in ample water to cover, or speed-soaked (page 24)

1 tablespoon olive oil

1 cup coarsely chopped onions

3 1/2 cups water

1/3 cup coarse bulgur

1 teaspoon caraway seeds

1/2 teaspoon crushed red pepper flakes, or more to taste

2 pounds eggplant, peeled and cut into 1-inch chunks (see Tip)

3 tablespoons tomato paste

2 tablespoons tahini (sesame seed paste)

1/2 cup hot or boiling water

2 to 3 cloves garlic, pushed through a press

2 teaspoons ground coriander seeds, or more to taste

1 1/4 teaspoons salt, or to taste

TOMATO-CUCUMBER SALAD

3 cups diced plum tomatoes (about 1 pound)

2 cups cucumbers, peeled, seeded, and diced (see Tip)

1/4 cup freshly squeezed lemon juice

1/2 cup chopped fresh cilantro or parsley

1 teaspoon salt

Drain the chickpeas and set aside.

Heat the oil in the cooker over medium-high heat. Cook the onions for 2 minutes, stirring frequently. Add the water, chickpeas, bulgur, caraway seeds, and red pepper flakes. Set the eggplant on top.

Lock the lid in place. Over high heat, bring to high pressure. Lower the heat just enough to maintain high pressure and cook for 16 minutes. While the stew is cooking, blend the tomato paste and tahini into the hot water. Set aside. Prepare the Tomato-Cucumber Salad by combining the tomatoes, cucumbers, lemon juice, cilantro, and salt in a large bowl. Set aside.

After 16 minutes, quick-release the pressure. Remove the lid, tilting it away from you to allow any excess steam to escape. Set the cooker over medium heat. Stir in the tomato paste mixture, garlic, coriander, and salt.

Stir well. If necessary, mash any remaining chunks of eggplant against the sides of the cooker and blend them in to create a thick, creamy sauce. Add more red pepper flakes and additional coriander, if needed. Cook over medium heat until the garlic loses its raw edge, about 3 minutes. Ladle portions of the stew into large, shallow bowls and sprinkle on a liberal portion of the Tomato-Cucumber Salad. Pass the remaining salad at the table.

SERVES 5 TO 6

TIP

If you use the long, thin Japanese eggplant, you don't have to peel it. Opt for seedless cucumbers or kirbies, which you don't have to seed.

CHICKPEAS IN EGGPLANT-TAHINI SAUCE WITH SPINACH

When you add the tomato paste, stir in about ¾ pound of thoroughly washed, chopped fresh spinach. Cook, uncovered, over medium heat until the spinach is tender, about 2 minutes.

NEW WORLD SUCCOTASH

This squash-orange stew unites the traditional American Indian combination of squash, lima beans, and corn with a few other New World discoveries, namely quinoa, tomatoes, and chile peppers. It's hard to imagine the great cuisines of the world without many of these treasured ingredients.

Be sure to use only large white lima beans in this recipe; they cook more quickly than other types because they have very thin skins. To keep the skins intact, soak and cook them in lightly salted water (a no-no for most other types of beans).

4 MINUTES UNDER PRESSURE

3 TO 4 MINUTES ADDITIONAL COOKING

1 cup **large dried white lima beans, picked over and rinsed, soaked overnight in ample water to cover plus ¼ teaspoon salt, or speed-soaked with salt (page 24)**

1 tablespoon **olive oil**

1 cup **coarsely chopped onions**

1 ½ teaspoons **whole cumin seeds**

2 cups **water**

½ cup **quinoa, thoroughly rinsed and drained**

½ teaspoon **salt, or more to taste**

2 pounds **kabocha squash, seeded and cut into 2-inch chunks, or butternut squash, peeled, quartered and seeded (see Tip)**

1 large **clove garlic, pushed through a press**

One 15-ounce **can diced tomatoes with green chiles or Mexican-style tomatoes, chopped, with liquid, or 2 cups finely chopped fresh tomatoes plus 1 to 2 jalapeños, seeded and finely chopped**

1 cup **fresh or frozen corn (rinse away any ice crystals)**

⅓ cup **chopped fresh cilantro**

1 tablespoon **freshly squeezed lime juice (optional)**

¼ cup **toasted pumpkin seeds (page 241), for garnish**

Drain the lima beans, discard any free-floating skins, and set aside.

Heat the oil in the cooker over medium-high heat. Cook the onions and cumin for 2 minutes, stirring frequently. Add the water, lima beans, quinoa, and salt. Set the squash on top.

Lock the lid in place. Over high heat, bring to high pressure. Lower the heat just enough to maintain high pressure and cook for 4 minutes. Quick-release the pressure by setting the cooker under cold water. Remove the lid, tilting it away from you to allow excess steam to escape. If the lima beans are not sufficiently tender, simmer with the lid set in place until done. (Remove the squash if you are concerned about overcooking it.)

Use a knife to slash the squash into smaller pieces. (You can do this right in the cooker.) Stir in the garlic, tomatoes, corn, and additional salt, if needed. Simmer over medium heat, stirring occasionally, until the garlic loses its raw taste and the flavors mingle, 3 to 4 minutes. Stir in the cilantro. Add lime juice, if you wish, to brighten the flavors. Garnish each serving with toasted pumpkin seeds.

SERVES 4

TIP

If you can find kabocha squash in your natural foods store, by all means use this delicious vegetable and don't even think of peeling it. A good alternative is butter-nut squash, which is tasty but needs to be peeled. Peeled butternut cooks faster than kabocha and tends to lose its shape, so it's best to cook it in larger pieces and cut it up after cooking.

ASIAN BEANS, BARLEY, AND BOK CHOY

Meaty dried shiitake mushrooms provide a deeply flavored stock for a stew that features small red Japanese adzuki beans, barley, and leafy green bok choy. These ingredients offer an appealing variety of colors and textures. The seasonings are typically Asian: fresh ginger, tamari soy sauce, scallions, and toasted sesame oil.

This is the ideal dish for an unpremeditated supper, since the beans and dried mushrooms require no presoaking and there is hardly any vegetable chopping required. If the stew seems slightly thin at first, just mash ½ cup of the beans against the side of the cooker and stir them in, or give it 15 minutes of standing time (or overnight refrigeration) and it will thicken right up.

18 MINUTES HIGH PRESSURE

5 MINUTES ADDITIONAL COOKING

7 cups water or 3 cups chicken broth and 4 cups water

1 cup adzuki beans, picked over and rinsed

½ cup pearl barley, rinsed

1 ounce (10 to 12 large) dried shiitake or Chinese black mushrooms

3 scallions, thinly sliced (keep white and green parts separate)

2 teaspoons toasted sesame oil, or more to taste

3 large carrots, peeled and halved crosswise

1 pound bok choy (4 large stalks), carefully rinsed and drained, cut in thirds lengthwise, then thinly sliced

1 tablespoon minced fresh ginger

3 tablespoons tamari or other Japanese soy sauce, or more to taste

2 to 3 teaspoons brown rice or seasoned rice vinegar

Salt (optional)

Bring the water to a boil in the cooker as you prepare and add the adzukis and barley. Snap the shiitake caps into small bits and add them to the pot. (If the shiitakes have stems, you may either reserve them for stock or grind them to a powder in a spice grinder and add them to the stew. Left whole, they remain very chewy.)

Add the sliced scallion bulbs and toasted sesame oil. (Do not be tempted to omit the oil as it controls the foaming action of the barley and beans.) Set the carrots on top.

Lock the lid in place. Over high heat, bring to high pressure. Lower the heat just enough to maintain high pressure and cook for 18 minutes. Quick-release the pressure by setting the cooker under cold running water. Remove the lid, tilting it away from you to allow any excess steam to escape. Transfer the carrots to a chopping board. If the beans are not close to tender, stir in another ½ to 1 cup water if the mixture seems dry, set (but do not lock) the lid in place, and cook until just about done.

Stir well as you add the bok choy, ginger, and tamari. Cook, covered, over medium-high heat, stirring occasionally, until the bok choy is tender-crisp, about 5 minutes. Add ½ cup of water during this time if the mixture seems dry. Cut the carrots into bite-sized pieces and stir them in.

Just before serving, stir in the scallion greens and add an extra ½ to 1 teaspoon toasted sesame oil, if needed. Stir in a bit of vinegar and salt or tamari to sharpen the flavors.

SERVES 4

GRAINS AND VEGETABLES

GRAINS AND VEGETABLES UNDER PRESSURE

Vegetables play an important supporting role in most of my recipes but in this chapter they steal the show.

Most vegetables and grains are done so quickly under pressure that cooking times hover around 4 minutes. It's an added bonus that since all of the water-soluble vitamins are captured in the cooking broth, these dishes are packed with good-for-you nutrients too.

Although I'd happily eat every dish in this chapter time and again, I'd like to call special attention to the risotto recipes. Years ago, a dinner guest watched me pressure-cook a mushroom risotto in 5 minutes and couldn't get over how closely it rivaled the taste and texture of the 30-minutes-of-stirring classic version.

"If I cook nothing else in that pot, it's worth the price," he said, and bought a pressure cooker at Zabar's (Mail-Order Sources, page 245) on the way home. Italian home cooks have told me that they always prepare risotto under pressure. Since you already have a cooker, there's nothing to stop you from having risotto for dinner tonight.

MINESTRONE

Every cook has a preferred version of this Italian favorite and here is mine, with its strong mushroom base.

This versatile recipe makes either a thick stew or a chunky soup, depending upon how much broth you add. It's very tasty whether you use cabbage or kale, although the latter offers more texture and color contrast.

A bowl of minestrone makes a filling dinner, but if you'd like an even heartier version—or want to stretch leftovers—ladle the soup over a slice of crisply toasted whole-grain bread that's been drizzled with olive oil and rubbed with the cut surface of a halved garlic clove.

4 MINUTES HIGH PRESSURE

2 MINUTES ADDITIONAL COOKING

½ ounce (½ cup loosely packed) dried mushrooms, preferably porcini

2 cups boiling water

1 tablespoon olive oil, or more if needed

1 cup coarsely chopped onions

2 to 4 cups chicken, beef, or vegetable broth

One 28-ounce can peeled plum tomatoes, with liquid

½ cup small pasta, such as elbows or ditalini

1 tablespoon Italian herb blend (page 238 or store-bought), or more to taste

½ teaspoon salt, or to taste

¼ teaspoon crushed red pepper flakes, or more to taste

Pinch of sugar

3 ribs celery, cut into ½-inch slices

3 carrots, peeled and cut into ½-inch slices

½ pound green or Savoy cabbage, shredded, or kale, stems thinly sliced and leaves coarsely chopped

1 to 2 large cloves garlic, pushed through a press

Freshly ground black pepper

1 cup freshly grated Parmesan cheese

continued

Set the mushrooms in a large glass measuring cup and pour the boiling water over them. Cover and set aside until soft, about 10 minutes. Remove the mushrooms with a slotted spoon and chop them coarsely if necessary. Set them and their soaking liquid aside separately.

Heat 1 tablespoon of oil in the cooker over medium-high heat. Cook the onions, stirring frequently, until they begin to soften, about 3 minutes. Add the broth, then pour the mushroom soaking liquid into the cooker, taking care to leave behind any residue on the bottom. Add the tomatoes and crush them against the side of the cooker with a large spoon. Add the pasta, soaked mushrooms, herb blend, salt, red pepper flakes, sugar, celery, and carrots and stir well. Set the cabbage on top. (Don't be concerned that it will reach almost to the top of the cooker; it will shrink dramatically as the cooker comes up to pressure.)

Lock the lid in place. Over high heat, bring to high pressure. (This may take as long as 5 minutes since the cooker is so full.) Reduce the heat just enough to maintain high pressure and cook for 4 minutes. Quick-release the pressure. Remove the lid, tilting it away from you to allow excess steam to escape.

Stir well as you add another tablespoon of oil (if needed to soften the tomatoes' acidity) and the garlic, taking care to release any pasta that may be stuck to the bottom of the cooker. Add more crushed red pepper, salt, and Italian herb blend, if you like. Add pepper to taste. Simmer until the garlic loses its raw taste and the vegetables and elbows are tender, about 2 minutes.

Sprinkle individual portions of the minestrone with a liberal dusting of Parmesan and pass the remaining cheese in a small bowl at the table.

SERVES 4 AS A STEW OR 5 TO 6 AS A SOUP

HEARTY BEAN MINESTRONE

Use 4 cups of broth and cook the soup with 1½ cups of cooked chickpeas, cannellini, or navy beans, or one 15-ounce can, drained and rinsed.

VARIATIONS

Substitute escarole or chicory for the cabbage.

Stir in ¼ cup chopped fresh basil or 1 tablespoon basil olive oil at the end.

PROVENÇAL VEGETABLE SOUP

What a fetching soup: saffron-golden with bright green flecks of zucchini and peas and the cheerful orange and red of chopped carrots and tomatoes. Beans thicken the soup and give it more substance.

All of the vegetables are harmonized by your choice of tarragon or the anise-infused spirit Pernod—both so characteristic of the Provençal region. (I prefer the sweet alcoholic edge of Pernod, but if you don't have it on hand, tarragon does nicely.) A bit of Parmesan stirred in at the end makes the whole much greater than the sum of its parts.

Serve the soup with a crusty loaf and the best goat cheese you can find.

12 MINUTES HIGH PRESSURE

6 MINUTES ADDITIONAL COOKING

1 cup cannellini, white kidney, or Great Northern beans, picked over and rinsed, then soaked overnight in ample water to cover, or speed-soaked (page 24)

1 tablespoon olive oil

2 cups thinly sliced leeks or coarsely chopped onions

4 cups chicken or vegetable broth, or half of each

1 cup diced celery

2 large carrots, peeled, halved lengthwise, and cut into 1/2-inch slices

One 15-ounce can diced tomatoes, or plum tomatoes, coarsely chopped, with liquid

1 1/2 tablespoons Pernod or 1 teaspoon dried tarragon, or more to taste

2 large cloves garlic, pushed through a press

1/2 teaspoon salt, or to taste

Generous 1/4 teaspoon saffron threads steeped in 2 tablespoons warm water

2 medium zucchini or yellow squash, quartered lengthwise and cut into 1/2-inch slices

1 cup frozen peas (rinse away any ice crystals)

1/2 cup freshly grated Parmesan

Drain and rinse the beans. Set aside.

Over medium-high heat, heat the oil in the cooker. Cook the leeks for 2 minutes, stirring frequently. Add the broth, reserved beans, celery, and carrots.

Lock the lid in place. Over high heat, bring to high pressure. Reduce the heat just enough to maintain high pressure and cook for 12 minutes. Quick-release the pressure. Remove the lid, tilting it away from you to allow excess steam to escape. If the beans are not tender, return them to high pressure for another 5 minutes.

Add the tomatoes, Pernod, garlic, salt, saffron (with steeping liquid), and zucchini. Cover and cook over medium heat until the zucchini are tender-crisp, about 5 minutes. If the soup seems too thin, mash about ½ cup of the beans against the side of the cooker with a fork and stir into the soup.

Stir in the peas and ¼ cup of the Parmesan. Add more salt, if needed. Cook, uncovered, over medium heat, stirring once or twice, until the peas are tender, about 1 minute. Serve in large bowls. Pass the extra Parmesan in a small bowl at the table.

SERVES 4

CHUNKY RATATOUILLE SOUP

Based on the ingredients typically used to make a traditional Provençal vegetable stew, this lovely soup is ideal for a light, warm-weather meal when basil and vine-ripened tomatoes are overflowing gardens and markets. The soup is good hot or cold.

The pressure cooker melts the eggplant and tomatoes into a chunky puree, creating the soup's liquid base. Shredded basil and orange zest offer a bright finish.

4 MINUTES HIGH PRESSURE

2 tablespoons olive oil

1 tablespoon minced garlic

2 cups thinly sliced leeks or coarsely chopped onions

2 cups vegetable broth or water

½ cup orzo, tubetti, or other small pasta

2 teaspoons dried oregano leaves

1 teaspoon whole fennel seeds

¼ teaspoon crushed red pepper flakes, or more to taste

1 teaspoon salt, or to taste

Pinch of sugar

1 pound eggplant, peeled and cut into 1-inch chunks (see Tips)

2 large red bell peppers, seeded and diced

1½ pounds plum tomatoes, peeled (see Tips) and coarsely chopped

1 cup tightly packed fresh basil leaves, snipped or cut into thin strips

½ teaspoon grated orange zest, or more to taste

1 to 2 teaspoons balsamic vinegar (optional)

Heat 1 tablespoon of the oil in the cooker over medium-high heat. Cook the garlic and leeks, stirring frequently, for 1 minute. Stir in the broth, orzo, oregano, fennel, red pepper flakes, salt, and sugar. Make sure that no bits of leek or garlic are sticking to the bottom of the cooker.

Add the eggplant and peppers, then set the tomatoes on top. *Do not stir.* (It's best to keep tomatoes away from the bottom of the pot, where their sugars can cause scorching.)

Lock the lid in place. Over high heat, bring to high pressure. Lower the heat just enough to maintain high pressure and cook for 4 minutes. Reduce pressure with a quick-release method. Remove the lid, tilting it away from you to allow any excess steam to escape.

Stir well, making sure that no orzo is sticking to the bottom of the pot. Press the eggplant against the side of the cooker with a large spoon and stir well to create a chunky puree. Add the remaining tablespoon of olive oil, the basil, orange zest, and additional red pepper flakes to taste. Stir in a bit of balsamic vinegar, if needed, to sharpen the flavors.

SERVES 4

TIPS

Small Japanese eggplants do not require peeling, but it's necessary to peel large eggplants and tomatoes, whose skins do not soften sufficiently in the cooker.

To peel tomatoes, first blanch them for 20 seconds in boiling water. With a slotted spoon, transfer them to a bowl of ice water. The peels will slip off easily. If you prefer, substitute one 28-ounce can of drained, peeled plum tomatoes.

WINTER VEGETABLE SOUP WITH BLACK BARLEY AND DILLED MUSTARD CREAM

If you haven't yet stocked your cupboard with black barley, you can make this soup with wheat berries, but I encourage you to mail-order black barley for its striking color, chewy texture, and nutty taste.

As the soup cooks, the cabbage becomes meltingly soft and thickens the broth. A simple Dilled Mustard Cream stirred in at the end gives the humble ingredients an aristocratic finish.

18 MINUTES UNDER PRESSURE

½ ounce (½ cup loosely packed) dried mushrooms

2 cups boiling water

1 tablespoon butter or vegetable oil

1 cup coarsely chopped onions

1 cup diced, peeled carrots

4 cups vegetable broth

½ cup dried black-eyed peas

½ cup black barley or wheat berries, rinsed

1 pound cabbage, shredded (about 6 cups)

2 large ribs celery, halved lengthwise and cut into ½-inch slices

2 large parsnips, peeled and cut into 1-inch chunks

½ teaspoon salt

DILLED MUSTARD CREAM

¾ cup sour cream

2 tablespoons Dijon mustard, preferably coarse grained (such as Maille à la Ancienne), or more to taste

3 tablespoons chopped fresh dill or 1½ teaspoons dried

1½ tablespoons freshly squeezed lemon juice, or more to taste

Freshly ground black pepper

Set the mushrooms in a small bowl and pour the boiling water on top. Cover and let steep until the mushrooms are soft, about 10 minutes.

Meanwhile, over medium-high heat, heat the butter in the cooker until it begins to foam. Add the onions and carrots and cook over medium heat, stirring frequently, until the vegetables are soft, about 5 minutes. Lower the heat if the vegetables begin to brown.

Lift the softened mushrooms out with a slotted spoon and chop coarsely if necessary. Pour the mushroom broth into the cooker, taking care to leave any sandy residue on the bottom of the bowl. Add the mushrooms, vegetable broth, black-eyed peas, and barley.

Lock the lid in place. Over high heat, bring to high pressure. Reduce the heat just enough to maintain high pressure and cook for 10 minutes. Quick-release the pressure under cold running water. Remove the lid, tilting it away from you to allow excess steam to escape. Stir in the cabbage, celery, parsnips, and salt. Return to high pressure and cook for an additional 8 minutes.

Meanwhile, prepare the Dilled Mustard Cream: In a medium bowl, blend together the sour cream, mustard, dill, and lemon juice. Add more mustard or lemon juice to taste.

After 8 minutes, quick-release the pressure by setting the cooker under cold running water. Remove the lid, tilting it away from you to allow excess steam to escape. Ladle out about ½ cup of the broth and blend in 2 tablespoons of the Mustard Cream. Stir this mixture back into the soup. Taste the soup and add a generous amount of pepper and more salt, if needed. Ladle the soup into large bowls and set a tablespoon of Mustard Cream in the center of each portion.

SERVES 5 TO 6

VEGETABLE STEW WITH ETHIOPIAN SPICES

This fragrant vegetable stew uses an Ethiopian blend of sweet and hot spices known as berbere (pronounced bari baray). Like an Indian curry powder, berbere includes the cook's own special blend of cardamom, cinnamon, cloves, cayenne, cumin, allspice, paprika, and black pepper, among other exotic spices. The blend often includes powdered ginger, but I've discovered that adding fresh ginger at the end results in superior taste.

Rutabaga (aka yellow turnip or swede) is the main vegetable in this stew, and if you've never tried it, rest assured that you're in for a terrific treat. Underneath its unappealing waxed exterior lies a tasty vegetable with a delicate orange hue. Take a look at the Guide to Ingredients (page 233) for instructions on cutting it up.

Peanut butter stirred in at the end enriches the sauce. Adding a garnish of chopped roasted peanuts may seem like gilding the lily, but it adds very appealing texture.

Ethiopians would sop up this stew with pieces of the tangy fermented flatbread called injera. Assuming that's not available, thin slices of fresh sourdough do nicely.

4 MINUTES HIGH PRESSURE

1 MINUTE ADDITIONAL COOKING

1 tablespoon butter or olive oil

1 1/2 teaspoons whole cumin seeds

1 1/2 cups coarsely chopped onions

4 tablespoons tomato paste

3 cups chicken or vegetable broth, or more if needed

1 teaspoon salt, or to taste

Generous 1/4 teaspoon each ground cinnamon and cardamom

1/8 teaspoon each cayenne, cloves, and freshly ground black pepper

1 1/2 pounds rutabaga, peeled and cut into 1/2-inch dice, or purple-topped turnips, peeled and cut into 1-inch chunks

1 pound red-skinned potatoes, scrubbed and cut into 1-inch chunks

5 large carrots, peeled and cut into 1-inch chunks

1 1/2 pounds green or Savoy cabbage, cored and coarsely chopped

6 tablespoons crunchy peanut butter (preferably unsalted and nonhydrogenated), at room temperature

1/2 cup hot water

1 1/2 tablespoons minced fresh ginger, or more to taste

1 cup frozen green peas (rinse away any ice crystals)

1/2 cup chopped roasted peanuts, for garnish

Over medium-high heat, heat the butter in the cooker until it begins to foam. Add the cumin seeds and cook, stirring frequently, until they turn a shade darker, about 30 seconds. Immediately stir in the onions and tomato paste and continue cooking for 2 minutes, stirring all the while.

Add the broth and take care to scrape up any browned bits sticking to the bottom of the cooker. Add the salt, spices, rutabaga, potatoes, and carrots. Pile the cabbage on top. (Don't be concerned if the cabbage reaches to the top of the cooker; it will quickly wilt as the mixture comes up to high pressure.)

Lock the lid in place. Over high heat, bring to high pressure. Reduce the heat just enough to maintain high pressure and cook for 4 minutes. Quick-release the pressure under cold running water. Remove the lid, tilting it away from you to allow excess steam to escape. If the vegetables are not sufficiently tender, set (but do not lock) the lid in place and cook over medium heat until done.

In a glass measuring cup, blend the peanut butter into the hot water. Stir in the ginger. Add this mixture to the stew. If the stew is too thick, stir in more broth. Adjust the seasonings, adding salt, additional berbere spices of your choice, and more fresh ginger, if desired.

Once you've got the seasonings just the way you want them, add the peas and cook just until tender but still bright green and crunchy, about 1 minute. Garnish individual portions with roasted peanuts.

SERVES 6

POTATO-CAULIFLOWER CURRY WITH MANGO YOGURT

In this homey curry, pale potatoes and cauliflower soften to a coarse flavorful mash. Against this comfort-food backdrop, bright dots of peas and tomatoes create quite a pretty dish.

Toasted brown mustard seeds add a nutty crunch and gentle bite, and a dollop of Mango Yogurt (made by blending sweet mango chutney into yogurt) provides an intense flavor contrast. Look for both mustard seeds and chutney in gourmet shops and Indian markets.

6 MINUTES HIGH PRESSURE

2 TO 3 MINUTES ADDITIONAL COOKING

1 ½ tablespoons brown mustard seeds

1 tablespoon butter, ghee, or peanut oil

2 teaspoons whole cumin seeds

1 ½ teaspoons fennel seeds

1 cup chicken or vegetable broth, or water

2 tablespoons mild curry powder (see Tips)

1 teaspoon salt, or to taste

¼ teaspoon cayenne, or more to taste (optional)

1 ½ pounds thin-skinned potatoes, such as Yukon Gold or red bliss, peeled or scrubbed, halved, and cut into ¼-inch slices (see Tips)

1 medium head cauliflower (about 2 ¼ pounds), trimmed and cut into large florets (about 2 inches across the top)

2 cups chopped fresh or canned (drained) plum tomatoes

1 cup frozen peas (rinse away any ice crystals)

1 tablespoon freshly squeezed lime juice, or more to taste

3 to 4 tablespoons chopped fresh cilantro, for garnish (optional)

MANGO YOGURT

1 heaping tablespoon sweet mango chutney

1 cup yogurt

Place the mustard seeds in the cooker. Set (but do not lock) the lid in place and turn the heat to high. When you hear the mustard seeds begin to pop (it will take about 1½ to 2 minutes), turn off the heat (move the cooker to a cool burner if your stove is electric), and leave the lid in place until the popping subsides. Transfer the toasted mustard seeds to a small bowl and set aside.

Heat the butter in the cooker. Add the cumin and fennel seeds and let them sizzle in the foaming butter for 20 seconds. Stir in the broth, curry powder, salt, and cayenne, if using. Add the potatoes and cauliflower and set the tomatoes on top. *Do not stir.*

Lock the lid in place. Over high heat, bring to high pressure. Reduce the heat just enough to maintain high pressure and cook for 6 minutes. Quick-release the pressure. Remove the lid, tilting it away from you to allow excess steam to escape. If the potatoes and cauliflower are not quite soft, set (but do not lock) the lid in place and allow them to steam in the residual heat for a minute or two.

Stir in the peas and reserved mustard seeds as you gently mix together the potatoes and cauliflower to create a coarse mash. Cook until the peas are tender-crisp, about 1 minute. Add salt to taste and a bit of lime juice to bring up the flavors.

To prepare the Mango Yogurt, in a small bowl blend the mango chutney and yogurt. Serve the curry in plates or large shallow bowls with a dollop of Mango Yogurt in the center. Garnish with cilantro, if you wish. Pass the remaining Mango Yogurt at the table.

SERVES 4

TIPS

Make sure that your curry powder is fresh and that you enjoy its taste. A personal favorite is Merwanjee Poonjiajee & Sons Madras curry sold in a gold tin. It's sold in Indian groceries and is also available from Adriana's Caravan and other mail-order sources (page 245).

I often leave the potato peels intact for added flavor, but the dish is softer without them. I leave the difficult choice to you. For variety, it's fun to use two types of potatoes.

NUTTY GRAIN SALAD WITH CURRANTS AND DILL

This colorful salad works well with most grains, but I particularly like to use a combination of barley and brown rice or wheat berries. The salad tastes best when the grains have been cooked in lightly salted water.

In this recipe, the natural nuttiness of the grains is accentuated by the nuts and a nut oil dressing. For optimum taste, let the dressed grains sit for about 15 minutes before serving. Pop any refrigerated leftovers into the microwave (lightly covered with waxed paper) for about 30 seconds to soften and rehydrate the grains. Then freshen the salad with additional lemon juice.

To round out the meal, mound individual portions on a bed of lightly dressed greens and surround with wedges of cheese—Brie is nice—and quartered apples or pears. Serve with a thinly sliced baguette.

4 to 5 cups freshly pressure-cooked grains (page 29)

2 cups grated carrots (from about 4 medium carrots)

1 cup snipped or finely chopped fresh dill (discard thick stems)

½ cup finely diced red onion or thinly sliced scallions

½ cup chopped toasted pecans or hazelnuts (page 239)

½ cup dried currants, briefly plumped in hot water

3 tablespoons walnut, hazelnut, or canola oil, or more to taste

3 tablespoons freshly squeezed lemon juice, or more to taste

½ teaspoon salt, or to taste

In a large bowl, combine all of the ingredients, adjusting the oil, lemon juice, and salt to your taste.

SERVES 4 TO 6

TEX-MEX GRAIN SALAD

Substitute ½ cup chopped fresh cilantro for the dill, toasted pumpkin seeds for the pecans (add them at the last minute to preserve crunchiness), and chopped pimento-stuffed olives for the currants. Dress with olive oil and freshly squeezed lime juice. Add salt and Tabasco sauce to taste.

TEX-MEX GRAIN AND BEAN SALAD

Follow the variation above. Add 1½ cups cooked black or pinto beans. Increase the amount of olive oil and lime juice to taste.

FRAGRANT VEGETABLE COUSCOUS

Cinnamon, cumin, and coriander suffuse this couscous with the haunting fla-vors of far-off places. In this context, nuggets of purple-topped turnips are a sweet surprise.

The recipe is made in two steps. First, the vegetables are briefly cooked under pressure until just short of tender. Then they are finished off as they steep with the couscous. The texture of the dish is slightly unpredictable, but it is usually moister (more stuffing-like) than a typical fluffy couscous.

Since the liquid ratio and cooking instructions differ from one brand of cous-cous to the next, check the package directions to figure out how much couscous is appropriate for 1½ cups of liquid. (For example, my brand calls for 1 cup of dry couscous for 1½ cups of liquid.) Avoid any brands that call for cooking the couscous rather than steeping it off the heat.

If you are using unsalted broth, you'll need a good teaspoon of salt to bring out the flavors in this dish. If using salted broth, reduce the amount of salt accord-ingly.

2 MINUTES HIGH PRESSURE

5 MINUTES FOR STEEPING

1 tablespoon olive oil

1½ teaspoons whole cumin seeds

1½ cups vegetable broth

2 tablespoons tomato paste

1 teaspoon salt, or to taste

1½ teaspoons sweet paprika

1 teaspoon ground cinnamon

A few twists of freshly ground black pepper

4 large carrots, peeled, halved lengthwise, and cut into ¾-inch slices

1 pound purple-topped turnips, peeled and cut into 1-inch dice, or rutabaga, peeled and cut into ½-inch dice

1½ cups cooked chickpeas or one 15-ounce can, drained and rinsed

2 teaspoons ground coriander seeds

⅓ cup dried currants or ½ cup dark raisins (plump them in hot water if they are dried out)

1 cup frozen green peas or petite peas (rinse away any ice crystals)

1 cup uncooked couscous, approximately (see headnote)

1 cup shelled pistachios or coarsely chopped toasted walnuts or almonds (or a combination)

Over medium-high heat, heat the oil in the cooker. Stir in the cumin seeds and cook, stirring frequently, until they turn a shade darker and emit a toasted aroma, 20 to 30 seconds. Add the broth, and blend in the tomato paste, salt, paprika, cinnamon, and black pepper. Add the carrots, turnips, and chickpeas.

Lock the lid in place. Over high heat, bring to high pressure. Reduce the heat just enough to maintain high pressure and cook for 2 minutes. Quick-release the pressure. If the vegetables are not just short of tender, set (but do not lock) the lid in place and cook them over medium heat for another minute or two.

Stir in the coriander and currants. Adjust the salt to your taste, keeping in mind that once the couscous absorbs the liquid, the saltiness will be more subdued. Over high heat, bring the mixture to a boil. Stir in the peas and couscous.

Set the lid in place, turn off the heat, and let the mixture sit until the couscous is tender, about 5 minutes. If all of the liquid has been absorbed but the couscous is not sufficiently tender, rapidly stir in ¼ cup boiling water, set the lid in place, and steam for a few minutes more. Alternatively, if the couscous is tender and there is unabsorbed liquid, drain it off. Stir in the nuts as you fluff up the couscous. Serve hot or at room temperature.

SERVES 4

A FEW WORDS ABOUT RISOTTO

In Northern Italy, rice reigns supreme and pasta takes second place. Once you've tasted risotto, you'll understand why. Like pasta, risotto can be prepared in an infinite number of ways, from simple to complex, using seasonal vegetables and varying the herbs and spices. When risotto is prepared by the classical method, broth is slowly added to the rice over a period of thirty minutes of almost constant stirring. Who can entertain guests while doing that?

Enter the pressure cooker: 4 minutes of unattended cooking, a few minutes of stirring at the end, and you're done. Because it is so simple to prepare and so versatile and sophisticated, risotto is likely to become standard company fare in your home as it has in mine.

However, before putting risotto on the menu, locate a source for the plump, medium-grained Italian white rice called arborio. When arborio is cooked in a generous quantity of broth, it releases a starchy substance, creating a luscious creamy sauce that envelopes each grain.

Arborio is nowadays available in many supermarkets and gourmet shops, or you can purchase it by mail order (page 245). Don't rinse the rice, as that would wash away some of the starch that makes the dish what it is.

Four simple recipes follow. You'll find additional risotto recipes using shrimp, smoked turkey, and lamb shanks by consulting the index.

Leftover Risotto

Although most connoisseurs shun leftover risotto, I think it tastes just dandy. If you reheat risotto, lightly covered, in a microwave it will regain its pleasing creaminess. If you don't own a microwave, shape the risotto into small, flat patties and brown them lightly in a little butter or olive oil in a nonstick pan.

RISOTTO WITH BUTTERNUT SQUASH AND SAGE

For a creamy risotto without the cream, this recipe can't be beat. The squash melts down into a puree, napping the kernels of rice in a thick pale-amber sauce. Like special friends, sage and squash bring out the best in each other.

4 MINUTES HIGH PRESSURE

3 TO 4 MINUTES ADDITIONAL COOKING

1 tablespoon butter or olive oil

1 cup minced onions

1½ cups arborio rice

½ cup dry white wine or dry vermouth

4 cups chicken or vegetable broth

1½ pounds butternut squash, peeled, seeded, and cut into 1-inch chunks (about 3 cups)

1 teaspoon salt, or to taste

Generous teaspoon dried sage leaves

½ cup freshly grated Parmesan cheese

3 tablespoons minced fresh parsley, for garnish

Heat the butter in the cooker over medium-high heat until it begins to foam. Cook the onions, stirring frequently, until they soften slightly, about 2 minutes. Stir in the rice, taking care to coat it with the oil. Add the wine and continue cooking and stirring until most of it has evaporated, about 1 minute. Add the broth, squash, and salt.

Lock the lid in place. Over high heat, bring to high pressure. Reduce the heat just enough to maintain high pressure and cook for 4 minutes. Quick-release the pressure by setting the cooker under cold running water. Remove the lid, tilting it away from you to allow excess steam to escape.

Crumble the sage leaves into the risotto. Boil over medium-high heat, stirring constantly, until the rice is tender but still chewy, most of the squash is pureed (a few small chunks here and there are fine), and the risotto loses most of its soupiness and becomes creamy and thick, 3 to 4 minutes. Turn off the heat and stir in the Parmesan and additional salt, if needed. Serve immediately in large shallow bowls garnished with parsley.

SERVES 4

RISOTTO WITH KABOCHA

Substitute unpeeled kabocha (page 238) for the butternut squash. The peel will soften nicely and the risotto will sport flecks of bright green.

PORCINI RISOTTO WITH ASPARAGUS

This is the recipe I turn to time and again when company is coming. It's luxurious and utterly delicious. The only problem is that people can't resist seconds and a recipe that should theoretically serve 6 often serves only 4. But it will serve 4 amply!

Red wine deepens the flavor and color of this risotto, accentuating the mushrooms' "beefy" taste. Porcini are so full of flavor that when asparagus is not in season, you can simply omit it and still have a terrific dish.

You'll find porcini in gourmet shops and through mail-order sources (page 245)— or substitute less expensive dried mushrooms for a weeknight family meal.

4 MINUTES HIGH PRESSURE

3 TO 4 MINUTES ADDITIONAL COOKING

1½ ounces (1½ cups loosely packed) dried porcini mushrooms

3 cups boiling water

1½ pounds asparagus, trimmed

1 tablespoon olive oil

1 tablespoon butter

¾ cups finely chopped shallots

2 cups arborio rice

½ cup dry red wine

2½ cups chicken or vegetable broth

1¼ teaspoons salt, or to taste

1 cup freshly grated Parmesan cheese, plus more to pass at the table

3 tablespoons minced fresh parsley, for garnish

Place the porcini in a medium bowl and pour the water on top. Cover and let sit until the mushrooms are soft, about 10 minutes. Meanwhile steam the asparagus in the cooker until tender-crisp, 3 to 5 minutes, depending on thickness. Run under cold water to set the color, then cut on a sharp diagonal into ½-inch slices. Set aside. Lift out the porcini with a slotted spoon and chop any large pieces. Set the mushrooms and soaking liquid aside separately.

continued

Rinse and dry off the cooker. Heat the oil and butter in the cooker over medium-high heat. Cook the shallots, stirring frequently, until softened slightly, about 2 minutes. Stir in the rice, taking care to coat it with the oil. Add the wine and continue cooking and stirring until most of it has evaporated, about 1 minute. Carefully pour in the mushroom broth, taking care to leave any sediment on the bottom of the bowl. Stir in the porcini, chicken broth, and salt.

Lock the lid in place. Over high heat, bring to high pressure. Reduce the heat just enough to maintain high pressure and cook for 4 minutes. Quick-release the pressure by setting the cooker under cold running water. Remove the lid, tilting it away from you to allow excess steam to escape.

Boil over medium-high heat, stirring constantly, until the rice is tender but still chewy and the risotto loses most of its soupiness and becomes creamy and thick, 3 to 4 minutes. Turn off the heat and stir in the asparagus, Parmesan, and salt, if needed. Serve immediately in large shallow bowls, garnished with parsley. Pass additional grated Parmesan at the table.

SERVES 4

RISOTTO WITH TOMATOES, OLIVES, AND SMOKED MOZZARELLA

Since I'm a great fan of both olives and smoked mozzarella, combining them in risotto was a sure way for me to create a boldly flavored dish I would love.

Make this tomato-red risotto with the best olives you can find. I like to use a combination of large green Sicilian and deep-purple Greek kalamatas, cooking one type with the rice so that its flavor permeates the dish, then stirring in the second variety at the end to give the risotto little pockets of intense flavor. You can use only one type of olive, if you prefer, and even cut the total amount in half if you're not as much of an olive nut as I.

Since olives are quite salty, it's safest to add salt, if you need it, at the end of cooking.

4 MINUTES HIGH PRESSURE

3 TO 4 MINUTES ADDITIONAL COOKING

1 tablespoon butter or olive oil

1 cup thinly sliced leeks or finely chopped onions

1½ teaspoons Italian herb blend (page 238 or store-bought)

¼ teaspoon crushed red pepper flakes, or more to taste

1½ cups arborio rice

½ cup dry white wine or dry vermouth

One 15-ounce can diced tomatoes, or plum tomatoes, coarsely chopped, with liquid

2½ cups chicken or vegetable broth

½ cup pitted kalamata or other Mediterranean black olives, pitted and halved

6 ounces smoked mozzarella, shredded (or substitute fresh mozzarella and add a drop or two of liquid smoke at the end)

½ cup Sicilian or other good-quality green olives, pitted and coarsely chopped

1 cup loosely packed fresh parsley leaves (no need to chop)

Salt to taste

continued

Heat the butter in the cooker over medium-high heat. When it begins to foam, add the leeks, herbs, and crushed red pepper and cook, stirring frequently, for 1 minute. Stir in the rice and coat it with the butter. Add the wine and cook over high heat, stirring, until it evaporates, about 1 minute. Add the tomatoes, broth, and black olives.

Lock the lid in place. Over high heat, bring to high pressure. Lower the heat to maintain high pressure and cook for 4 minutes. Quick-release the pressure by setting the cooker under cold running water. Remove the lid, tilting it away from you to allow any excess steam to escape.

Boil over medium-high heat, stirring constantly, until the rice is tender but still chewy and the risotto loses most of its soupiness and becomes creamy and thick, 3 to 4 minutes. Turn off the heat and stir in the smoked mozzarella, green olives, parsley, and salt, if needed. Continue to stir just until the mozzarella has softened and the parsley becomes limp, about 30 seconds. Serve in large shallow bowls.

SERVES 3 TO 4

RISOTTO WITH GREEN PEAS

Known by Italians as risi e bisi (bisi means peas in the Venetian dialect), this risotto is based on ingredients I always keep on hand for a last-minute supper. Don't be fooled by the recipe's simplicity: Risi e bisi is elegant, colorful, and tasty enough to offer to company. For a nice change, try using the small green peas called petits pois.

4 MINUTES HIGH PRESSURE

3 TO 4 MINUTES ADDITIONAL COOKING

1 tablespoon butter or olive oil
1½ cups chopped leeks or onions
1½ cups arborio rice
½ cup dry white wine, dry vermouth, or dry sherry
4 cups chicken or vegetable broth
1 teaspoon salt, or to taste
One 10-ounce package frozen peas (rinse away any ice crystals)
¾ cup freshly grated Parmesan cheese, plus more to pass at the table
2 teaspoons good-quality balsamic vinegar, or more to taste (optional)
Freshly ground black pepper

Heat the butter in the cooker over medium-high heat. When it begins to foam, add the leeks and cook for 1 minute, stirring frequently. Stir in the rice and coat the grains with the butter. Add the wine and cook over high heat, stirring, until it evaporates, about 1 minute. Add the broth and salt.

Lock the lid in place. Over high heat, bring to high pressure. Lower the heat to maintain high pressure and cook for 4 minutes. Quick-release the pressure by setting the cooker under cold running water. Remove the lid, tilting it away from you to allow any excess steam to escape.

Boil over medium-high heat, stirring constantly, until the rice is tender but still chewy and the risotto loses most of its soupiness and becomes creamy and thick, 3 to 4 minutes. During the final minute, stir in the peas and Parmesan. Add balsamic vinegar, if needed, to bring up the flavors.

Spoon the risotto into large shallow bowls and sprinkle with a few twists of black pepper. Pass extra Parmesan at the table.

SERVES 3 TO 4

JUST DESSERTS

DESSERTS UNDER PRESSURE

Desserts in a pressure cooker? Tasting is believing, and you certainly deserve a few special treats after qualifying as a one-pot-meal enthusiast.

The cooker does a terrific job of quick-steaming traditional favorites like bread pudding and cheesecake. The puddings are made in a 1½-quart soufflé dish (or other heatproof casserole) and the cheesecake in a 7-inch springform pan. Both are wrapped in heavy-duty aluminum foil and then set on a rack over water. (If a rack didn't come with your cooker, you can improvise one; see page 4.)

That's it for special equipment. None needed for making rice pudding and, if you've already tried the risotto, you can easily believe that the cooker serves forth a creamy rendition of this American classic in record time. A light and simple winter fruit compote brings this bonus chapter to a sweet close.

BLACK AND WHITE CHEESECAKE

Here's your recipe for a sinfully rich chocolate-marbled cheesecake. There's no bottom crust to worry about, and it's quick to assemble. The cheesecake sometimes emerges from the cooker looking rustic, with some peaks and valleys on top, but the taste is dependably urbane.

I like the texture best when it's served freshly prepared and slightly warm, even though you can't cut it into tidy slices. It gets firmer and denser—like a New York–style cheesecake—after overnight refrigeration. For optimum flavor, bring it back to room temperature before serving.

The cheesecake freezes beautifully and can be popped straight from the freezer into the microwave for a quick defrost—about 20 seconds on high for a slice.

You'll need a 7-inch springform pan to prepare this recipe. If your local kitchen store doesn't carry one, you can mail-order the pan from Zabar's (page 246). For a few more pointers, check the Tips below.

35 MINUTES HIGH PRESSURE PLUS 15-MINUTE NATURAL PRESSURE RELEASE

1 teaspoon butter at room temperature, for greasing the springform pan
20 ounces cream cheese, at room temperature
1 cup sugar
2 tablespoons all-purpose flour
4 large or extra-large eggs
½ cup sour cream
1¼ teaspoons pure vanilla extract
3 ounces good-quality bittersweet chocolate, melted and slightly cooled

Grease the springform pan with butter and set aside.

Using a hand blender or food processor, blend the cream cheese, sugar, and flour for about 15 seconds. Add the eggs, sour cream, and vanilla and blend until smooth, about 10 seconds more. Do not overwork the batter.

continued

Blend 1 cup of batter into the melted chocolate. Pour all of the remaining batter into the prepared pan. Gently drop tablespoonsful of the chocolate batter into the cheesecake in evenly spaced circles. Firmly swirl the flat side of a knife through the batter in 8 to 10 figure-eight motions to create a marbled effect.

Set the pan in the middle of a large sheet of heavy-duty aluminum foil about 2 feet long. Bring the two longer ends up to meet, and fold over to seal, creating a "tent" to allow some space on top for the cheesecake to puff up. Bring the short ends of the foil together and press them tightly against the sides of the pan.

Set a trivet or steaming rack on the bottom of the cooker. Lower the cheesecake into the cooker. Pour in enough water to reach halfway up the sides of the springform pan.

Lock the lid in place. Over high heat, bring to high pressure. Reduce the heat just enough to maintain high pressure and cook for 35 minutes. Turn off the heat and allow the pressure to drop naturally, about 15 minutes. Remove the lid, tilting it away from you to allow excess steam to escape.

Let the cheesecake cool for a few minutes before removing it from the cooker. Set it on a cooling rack, remove the foil, and let it cool slightly. Serve warm with a spoon or cool to room temperature, cover, and refrigerate at least 6 hours or overnight. Before serving, let the cheesecake come to room temperature, remove the springform pan, and cut into slices.

SERVES 8

TIPS

- Don't substitute reduced-fat products in this recipe as they contain more water and the cheesecake won't set properly.

- Bring the cream cheese to room temperature so that it will easily blend into the other ingredients.

- Use a fine-eating bittersweet chocolate bar, not baking chocolate.

- If there's a tiny puddle of water in the middle when you unwrap the cheesecake, gently sop it up with a paper towel.

LEMON CHEESECAKE

Omit the vanilla extract and chocolate, and blend the zest of 2 lemons (about 1 tablespoon) into the entire batch of batter. Garnish the whole cheesecake or individual slices with raspberries, blueberries, or sliced strawberries, if you wish.

BLUEBERRY BREAD PUDDING

This down-home bread pudding is a snap to throw together and can be made with fresh or frozen (not thawed) blueberries. It's a treat for dessert, but you can also keep it in mind for the entrée at your next brunch.

The pudding is steamed in a 1½-quart soufflé or other ovenproof casserole. I usually prepare the pudding right in the soufflé, but you might find it easier to use a large mixing bowl and then transfer it. Although it's not a fussy recipe, the texture is most appealing when you use a dense bread, such as a good-quality French or Italian white or whole-wheat loaf. Cut the bread into ½-inch slices, then into cubes. Spread on a large platter to dry out overnight. Remove the crusts, if you wish; the pudding is more rustic when they're left on.

You may serve the pudding warm, straight out of the cooker, but the fruit flavor deepens and the custardy texture improves after a 24-hour sojourn in the refrigerator. For future reference, try serving this dessert both ways and see which you prefer. Either way, serve it chilled with sweetened whipped cream.

35 MINUTES HIGH PRESSURE PLUS 10-MINUTE NATURAL PRESSURE RELEASE

4 large or extra-large eggs
¾ cup milk or half-and-half
⅓ cup sugar
1 teaspoon pure vanilla extract
¼ teaspoon ground cinnamon
3 cups loosely packed ½-inch cubes stale bread
1¾ cups fresh blueberries or 12 ounces frozen (not thawed)
Sweetened whipped cream, for garnish

In a 1½-quart soufflé or other heatproof dish that fits into the cooker, lightly beat the eggs with a whisk or fork. Blend in the milk, sugar, vanilla, and cinnamon.

Gently stir in the bread cubes, taking care to coat thoroughly with the liquid. Stir in the blueberries. Press the contents down gently to even off the top.

Set the pudding dish in the middle of a sheet of heavy-duty aluminum foil about 2 feet long. Bring the two longer ends up to meet, and fold over to seal, creating a "tent" to allow some space on top for the pudding to puff up. Bring the short ends of the foil together and press them tightly against the sides of the dish.

Set a trivet or steaming rack on the bottom of the cooker. Lower the pudding into the cooker. Pour in enough water to reach halfway up the sides of the pudding dish.

Lock the lid in place. Over high heat, bring to high pressure. Reduce the heat just enough to maintain high pressure and cook for 35 minutes. Let the pressure drop naturally for 10 minutes. Release any remaining pressure. Remove the lid, tilting it away from you to allow excess steam to escape.

When the steam has subsided, carefully lift the pudding out of the cooker and set it on a cooling rack. If serving warm, remove the foil, dish out, and garnish with whipped cream. Otherwise, cool to room temperature and refrigerate until needed.

SERVES 4 TO 6

RASPBERRY BREAD PUDDING

Substitute fresh or frozen raspberries for the blueberries.

CHOCOLATE BREAD PUDDING

There's a lot to be said for bread and chocolate! Here's a fudgy, rich bread pudding—a chocoholic's delight if I ever tasted one. When served warm, my favorite way, the texture is light and moist. Chilled, the flavor and texture are more intense. Either way, top each serving with a snowy peak of whipped cream or vanilla ice cream.

The recipe calls for both cocoa powder and chocolate morsels. For optimum taste, use a high-quality cocoa, such as Droste. Adding a bit of coffee tricks the palate by intensifying the chocolate taste.

As with the previous recipe, you'll need a 1½-quart soufflé dish that fits into the cooker, and some heavy-duty aluminum foil to cover it.

30 MINUTES HIGH PRESSURE PLUS 10-MINUTE NATURAL PRESSURE RELEASE

½ cup unsweetened cocoa powder

⅓ cup hot strong coffee, or ⅓ cup hot water plus ½ teaspoon instant coffee powder

6 large or extra-large egg yolks

1½ cups half-and-half

½ cup sugar

4 cups loosely packed ½-inch cubes stale, crustless bread

1 cup semi-sweet chocolate morsels

Sweetened whipped cream or ice cream, for garnish

Chopped toasted almonds (page 239), for garnish

Place the cocoa in a large bowl and dribble the coffee over it. Run a fork through the mixture a few times to begin incorporating the cocoa powder. Add the egg yolks, half-and-half, and sugar, and use a hand mixer or whisk to blend the mixture thoroughly.

Place one-third of the bread cubes in a 1½-quart soufflé or other heatproof dish that fits in the cooker. Pour one-third of the cocoa mixture over the bread cubes and distribute one-third of the morsels on top. Repeat this process twice more. With a fork or your fingers, gently press the top layer of bread cubes into the liquid until they become deeply colored.

Set the pudding dish in the middle of a large sheet of heavy-duty aluminum foil about 2 feet long. Bring the two longer ends up to meet and fold over several times to seal, allowing some space on top for the pudding to puff up. Bring the short edges of the foil together and press them tightly against the sides of the dish.

Set a trivet or steaming rack on the bottom of the cooker. Gently lower the pudding dish onto the trivet. Pour in enough water to reach halfway up the sides of the pudding dish.

Lock the lid in place. Over high heat, bring to high pressure. Reduce the heat just enough to maintain high pressure and cook for 30 minutes. Let the pressure drop naturally for 10 minutes, then quick-release any remaining pressure. Remove the lid, tilting it away from you to allow excess steam to escape.

When the steam has subsided, carefully lift the pudding out of the cooker and set it on a cooling rack. If serving warm, remove the foil, dish out, and garnish with whipped cream and toasted almonds. Otherwise, cool to room temperature and refrigerate until needed.

SERVES 6 TO 8

CHOCOLATE GRAND MARNIER BREAD PUDDING

Use 1¼ cups half-and-half and ¼ cup Grand Marnier or other orange liqueur.

RICE PUDDING

I couldn't be more pleased than I am with this pressure-cooker version of rice pudding—every bit as creamy as the traditional stovetop version that takes about an hour—here, yours in under 15 minutes. I've added the tablespoon of butter to keep the rice from foaming as it cooks, so don't be tempted to omit it.

The pudding may seem soupy at first, but it quickly thickens as it sits. You can serve it straight from the pot or spoon steaming-hot portions into individual ramekins. Refrigerate well covered for up to 5 days, or freeze, and then reheat in the microwave as needed. Before reheating, pour about $^1/_4$ cup milk or water per portion over leftovers. Heat thoroughly, then stir until nice and creamy. For a special treat, top each portion with some Winter Fruit Compote (page 232).

8 MINUTES HIGH PRESSURE

5 MINUTES ADDITIONAL COOKING

3 cups whole milk or half-and-half

3 cups water

$^1/_2$ cup sugar, or more to taste

$^1/_8$ teaspoon salt

1 $^1/_2$ cups extra-long-grain white rice

1 tablespoon sweet butter

$^1/_2$ teaspoon ground cinnamon (optional)

1 teaspoon pure vanilla extract, or more to taste

Few gratings of nutmeg

Ground cinnamon and/or $^1/_3$ cup chopped toasted almonds (page 239), for garnish (optional)

Place the milk, water, sugar, salt, rice, butter, and cinnamon, if using, in the cooker. Stir once or twice.

Lock the lid in place. Over high heat, bring to high pressure. Reduce the heat just enough to maintain high pressure and cook for 8 minutes. Quick-release the pressure by setting the cooker under cold running water. Remove the lid, tilting it away from you to allow excess steam to escape.

Stir well as you add vanilla and nutmeg to taste. Add more sugar, if needed. Cook, uncovered, over low heat at a gentle boil, stirring frequently, for 5 minutes. For a thicker pudding, cover and let sit for about 30 minutes. Reheat before serving. If you wish, dust with cinnamon and/or sprinkle toasted almonds on top.

SERVES 6 TO 8

RUM-RAISIN RICE PUDDING

Omit the cinnamon and cook the pudding as directed above. After releasing the pressure, stir in ½ cup dark or golden raisins and 2 to 3 tablespoons rum. Proceed as directed.

MAPLE WALNUT RICE PUDDING

Substitute maple syrup for the sugar. Omit the cinnamon and nutmeg. Stir in 1 cup chopped toasted walnuts after cooking.

COCONUT MILK RICE PUDDING

Omit the dairy milk and use one 14-ounce can coconut milk and 4 cups water. Substitute ground cardamom for the cinnamon; after releasing the pressure add it along with ¾ cup snipped dried mangoes or apricots, if you wish. Use chopped pistachio nuts for garnish.

REDUCED-FAT RICE PUDDING

Use 6 cups skim milk or 2 percent instead of whole milk and water. The pudding will not be as rich, but will still thicken nicely.

WINTER FRUIT COMPOTE WITH PORT

A simple and soothing dessert, given a touch of class with a lacing of port. You can vary the recipe by using rum, Madeira, or an almond or orange liqueur. You'll need no added sugar since the fruit is so sweet. The compote is nice on its own and also makes a fine topping for ice cream, rice pudding, or a slice of pound cake.

4 MINUTES HIGH PRESSURE

2 cups water

¼ cup port, or more to taste

¼ teaspoon ground cinnamon, or more to taste

¼ teaspoon ground cardamom, or more to taste

4 large apples, peeled, cored, and cut into eighths

4 large ripe pears, peeled, cored, and cut into eighths

1 cup pitted prunes

1 cup dried apricots or ½ cup golden raisins

Grated zest of 1 small lemon

2 tablespoons freshly squeezed lemon juice, or more to taste

In the cooker, combine the water, port, cinnamon, and cardamom. Add the apples, pears, prunes, and apricots.

Lock the lid in place. Over high heat, bring to high pressure. Reduce the heat just enough to maintain high pressure and cook for 4 minutes. Quick-release the pressure. Remove the lid, tilting it away from you to allow excess steam to escape.

If the fruit is not sufficiently tender, simmer over medium heat, covered, until done. Gently stir in lemon zest and juice to taste. Add more port and spices, if you wish. Serve at room temperature or refrigerate for up to 4 days.

SERVES 6

GUIDE TO INGREDIENTS

This guide provides basic information about the selection and handling of most of the ingredients I use in the recipes. (You'll find details on individual meats and poultry at the beginning of those chapters.) In many cases, I've suggested sources, brands, and suitable substitutes. Check the listing of Mail-Order Sources (pages 245–246) for items available through catalogs.

Adzuki (aduki, azuki) beans: small reddish-brown Japanese beans with a slender white stripe down one side. They have a full, rich taste and cook relatively quickly without presoaking. Many people find adzukis more digestible than other beans. Available in health-food stores and Asian markets.

Anchovies: tiny, salt-cured, filleted Mediterranean fish that virtually dissolve during cooking, adding saltiness, enhanced flavor, and a hint of fishiness to the dish. Choose flat (not rolled) anchovies packed in olive oil. Refrigerate leftovers submerged in oil in a glass jar; they will last for months.

Andouille sausage: a spicy, smoked Cajun sausage traditionally made of chitterlings and tripe. If not available, substitute a spicy smoked sausage such as kielbasa.

Annatto oil: used widely in Latin American cooking, annatto oil adds earthy taste and rich, burnished color to foods. It is simple to prepare at home. Buy annatto seeds (often labeled "*achiote*") from a Hispanic market or Penzeys (Mail-Order Sources) and steep 1 tablespoon of them in ¼ cup olive oil over very low heat for 5 minutes. Cool, then pour through a fine-meshed strainer. Discard the seeds and refrigerate the oil in a tightly sealed container until needed. Lasts for at least 6 months.

Arborio rice: a short-grained "chubby" Italian rice with a high starch content that is a good choice for making classic risotto. Other excellent choices are *carnarole* and *vialone nanno,* both of which take slightly longer to cook. If your supermarket doesn't carry one of these varieties, look for them in gourmet shops or order by mail.

Balsamic vinegar: an aged wine vinegar from Modena, Italy. Quality and flavor vary widely from strongly acidic to smooth and mildly sweet. I prefer the latter type and recommend Cavalli brand, available in gourmet shops or by mail from Zingerman's.

Barbecue sauce: great to have on hand for last-minute meals, but be sure to find a brand whose first ingredient is tomato paste and not vinegar, or you'll find it too strong for these recipes. Bull's Eye Original is a brand that brings good results.

Barley: all recipes have been tested with pearl barley, not the longer-cooking pot barley, which has its outer layer of hull still intact. In supermarkets, pearl barley is simply labeled "barley"; look for it in the Hispanic section under the Goya label. Do not make the mistake of purchasing toasted barley.

Barley, black: a dark-skinned variety of barley native to Ethiopia with a nutty taste and chewy texture. Available by mail from Gold Mine Natural Food Co. or Indian Harvest.

Beef broth: if you're not using homemade, look for Perfect Addition (page 13), a good-tasting frozen concentrate available in many gourmet markets, or use a reduced-sodium canned broth. Modify added salt accordingly.

Bell pepper: see Red bell pepper, roasted.

Bok choy: a striking Chinese cabbage with broad ivory stems and billowing green leaves. Wash each stalk carefully to rinse away sand.

Broccoli rabe (raab, rape, rapini): a strong-tasting green with a slightly bitter edge and small buds that resemble broccoli florets. Look for bunches with vibrant color and no yellowing leaves.

Bulgur: wheat berries whose hulls and bran have been removed. The grains are then steamed, dried, and crushed into dark-brown grit-like pieces available in different grinds, from coarse to fine. Use coarse or medium bulgur for these recipes. Available under the Goya label in many supermarkets, or look in the bulk bins of health-food stores. For instructions on cooking bulgur, see page 33.

Calabaza: a large West Indian pumpkin with delicate pale orange flesh that somewhat resembles butternut squash, a good substitute. Calabaza is usually sold in wedges in markets that cater to a Hispanic population.

Cannellini beans: ivory, oval-shaped beans prized in Italy for their creamy texture and full flavor. You'll find them in international and gourmet markets, or substitute Great Northern or white kidney beans.

Capers: pickled flower buds that add an intense punch to sauces and salads. They come in various sizes, steeped in brine or salted. I favor the brined variety in the relatively small nonpareil size.

Chicken broth: if you're not using homemade, good options are the frozen Perfect Addition frozen concentrate (page 13) or Pacific Foods asceptic-packed free-range chicken broth, now available in supermarkets and health-food stores. If using canned broth, opt for the reduced-sodium version.

Chicory: a curly-leaved, bitter green much loved by Italians. When cooked, the bitterness fades considerably. If not available, substitute escarole.

Chili powder: a seasoning blend of oregano, cumin, garlic, and ground chiles that can range from mild to very hot, depending upon the type of chile peppers used. Since blends vary dramatically, for best results use one you're fond of and replace every six months or so, when its flavor has faded. To avoid a tongue lashing, I use a mild chili blend mail-ordered from Penzeys and then add heat to taste with crushed red pepper flakes, cayenne, or Tabasco sauce.

Chipotle chile: dried, smoked jalapeño with a fair amount of heat. Wear rubber gloves when handling. Available in gourmet shops and from Penzeys.

Chorizo: a chile-hot, highly seasoned pork sausage available in both fresh and dry versions. Used in both Spanish and Mexican cooking, fresh chorizo should be eaten within a few days, while dried chorizo may be refrigerated for 2 weeks or longer, depending upon how it was cured. You may use either type in the recipes; fresh chorizo should be cooked along with the other ingredients and dried chorizo may be diced and stirred in at the end.

Cilantro (Chinese parsley, fresh coriander leaves): a highly aromatic herb that looks a bit like flat-leaf Italian parsley but has broader, lacier leaves. It is adored by many, and detested by some who find its taste "soapy." (For these pitiable folks, you may substitute parsley.) Refrigerate cilantro, stems submerged in water, and leaves covered with a plastic bag. Dried cilantro leaves are not worth using.

Coconut, dried: desiccated, unsweetened, grated coconut adds richness and a bit of crunch. It is sold in Indian markets and health-food stores. Most dried coconut available in supermarkets has been sweetened and is not suitable for savory dishes. To avoid rancidity, store dried coconut in a tightly sealed container in the freezer.

Coconut milk: a luscious, rich liquid extracted from fresh coconut, readily available in cans. Be sure to use the unsweetened product and avoid anything labeled "coconut cream." Avoid watered-down "lite" coconut milk unless the recipe specifies it.

Collards (collard greens): large, elephant ear–shaped greens, a mainstay of the southern kitchen and a fine source of calcium. Don't discard the thick midribs, which quickly become tender under pressure.

Couscous: a grain-shaped pasta made of semolina (durum wheat stripped of bran and germ) that needs no more than a brief steeping in boiling water. When preparing couscous recipes, avoid brands that require cooking, and check package directions for precise timing and proportions of liquid to dry couscous.

Cremini mushrooms: cultivated mushrooms whose shape resembles the common button variety, but which are darker and more flavorful. They hold their shape extremely well in cooking. If not using immediately, refrigerate in a basket lightly draped with a paper towel, or pack loosely in a paper bag.

Cumin seeds: tiny brown seeds with a woodsy character that predominate in Mexican and Middle Eastern cooking; recipes call for whole cumin seeds, which retain their flavor better than ground cumin under pressure.

Currants (dried): the dried fruit of Zante grapes, smaller and less sweet than raisins, and therefore ideal for grain salads and other savory dishes.

Curry powder: a blend of spices that varies dramatically from one cook or manufacturer to the next, but usually contains cumin, coriander, and mustard seeds, as well as fenugreek, red chiles, black peppercorns, and turmeric (the spice that turns curries yellow). My recipes call for a mild curry powder, and I recommend the very tasty Madras Curry Powder made by Merwanjee Poonjiajee & Sons, sold in small tins and available in gourmet shops and by mail from Adriana's Caravan.

Delicata squash: a cucumber-shaped winter squash with bright yellow skin and green or deep orange stripes. Delicata makes a nice substitute for butternut squash; its peel softens nicely under pressure and its orange flesh is sweet and dense. You'll usually find organic delicata in health-food stores and it's "cropping up" more in supermarkets.

Escarole: a slightly bitter green much favored by Italians. Its shape vaguely resembles romaine lettuce, but its leaves are much darker. Rinse carefully to remove sand.

Fennel seeds: plump, brownish-green ridged seeds with a distinct anise flavor.

Fish broth: if you're not preparing homemade, good options are frozen Perfect Addition (page 13) or bottled clam juice.

Garlic: The flavor of garlic disappears under pressure, no matter how much you add, so it makes sense to stir it in at the end. Pushing the cloves through a garlic press mashes the flesh and distributes the flavor efficiently when the garlic is added a few minutes before serving. *To roast garlic:* Do not separate the cloves. Remove as much of the papery skin from the head as you can. Set the head in a small shallow baking dish in a toaster oven or standard oven and roast at 375°F until the outside is lightly browned and the innermost cloves are very soft, about 20 minutes. To use, squeeze the very soft flesh from individual cloves. Refrigerate leftover unpeeled cloves in a sealed container for up to 2 weeks.

Ghee: clarified butter which has a high smoking point (which means that it won't burn as readily as butter that still contains milk solids); available in Indian groceries and by mail from Adriana's Caravan. Lasts indefinitely in the refrigerator.

Ginger: look for fresh, firm knobs with smooth skins. Peel or rinse and trim the amount you need. Figure on using almost twice as much when grating as when mincing, since much of the fiber gets separated and discarded when grating and the finer pieces pack more tightly into a measuring spoon. (For example, a 1-inch chunk yields about 1 tablespoon minced and 1½ teaspoons grated.) I usually mince ginger when it will be cooked and grate it for adding at the last minute. Dried ground ginger has quite a different flavor and does not make a good substitute.

Herbs (dried): for optimum flavor, best purchased in small quantities and in leaf (as opposed to ground) form. Store in a glass bottle in a cool, dry place away from the light, and replenish every six months or so. For a real treat, mail-order dried herbs from Penzeys.

Herbs (fresh): Refrigerate long-stemmed herbs (such as parsley, cilantro, and dill) with their roots submerged in water and their leaves covered with a plastic bag for up to 1 week. Refrigerate herbs on thin twig-like stems (such as fresh oregano, rosemary, and thyme) in zipper-topped plastic bags for up to 10 days.

Hominy, cracked: the coarsely chopped kernels of a starchy variety of white or yellow corn, known in Spanish as *posole*. When cooked, they maintain a chewy texture and have a delicate corn flavor. Available in supermarkets under the Goya label.

Italian herb blend: found among the spice jars in your supermarket, but it's tasty and simple to make your own by combining 1 tablespoon each dried oregano and basil leaves, 2 teaspoons each dried thyme and rosemary leaves, and 1½ teaspoons fennel seeds. Add 1 teaspoon crushed red pepper flakes, if you wish. Store in a small bottle in a cool, dark place.

Italian sausage: a fresh sausage made primarily of ground pork and seasonings, including fennel seeds. It will be labeled either "sweet" (containing a mix of herbs and spices) or "spicy" (seasonings including chile peppers). Store under refrigeration and cook thoroughly before eating. It is not necessary to remove the casing unless you are planning to crumble the meat.

Kabocha (Hokkaido pumpkin): a delicious winter squash that looks like the buttercup variety, but is denser, starchier, and more intensely flavored. The cooked peel becomes tender enough to eat. Look for it in the organic section of supermarkets and health-food stores.

Kalamata olives: large, purplish-black Greek olives with assertive flavor. Usually available in bulk anywhere good olives are sold, but you'll also find them in jars in many supermarkets.

Kale: a hearty winter green with curly leaves. Trim off the root end and chop as directed in the recipe. Wash well to remove sand that lodges in the leaves.

Kielbasa (kielbasy, Polish sausage): This garlicky pork sausage is sold either fresh or lightly smoked. Unless the package is labeled "precooked," it must be cooked thoroughly before eating.

Leeks: delicious cousins to the onion, which add terrific flavor to soups and stews. Remove and discard any bruised outer leaves. Trim off and discard the root end. Slice the remaining white and light green parts (save the dark top part of the leaves for making broth), and separate the rings. Rinse well in several changes of water to release all sand; drain thoroughly.

Lemongrass: a long greenish stalk with a small bulb at the bottom and a pungent taste and aroma reminiscent of lemon zest. Peel off and discard any tough outer layer, then smash, slice, or chop the fleshy bulb. Freeze whole stalks tightly wrapped in plastic and aluminum foil for up to 3 months. If fresh lemongrass is not available, Thai Kitchen's jarred lemongrass makes an acceptable substitute. Dried lemongrass is not recommended.

Lemon zest: the yellow peel that contains flavor-packed oils. You may zest a lemon by using the finest side of a box grater, but you will get more zest per lemon if you remove the peel in strips with a sharp old-fashioned potato peeler, using a gentle sawing motion. (Avoid scraping off the white layer of pith underneath the yellow as it is bitter.) Mince the peel by hand or use a minichopper.

Linguiça: a garlic-infused, spicy Portuguese sausage similar to chorizo, which may be used in its place.

Liquid smoke: a bottled seasoning that imparts the flavor of hickory or mesquite. Available in most supermarkets. Use with discretion; a drop or two will flavor a dish that serves four.

Mint: a refreshing herb much used in Middle Eastern cooking. Make sure to use spearmint and not peppermint, which will make your dish taste like toothpaste or candy. If you usually stock spearmint tea bags in the house, you can snip open the bag and use the dried leaves.

Mushrooms, dried: unless specified, use any variety that you prefer, including porcini from Italy or the less expensive but very flavorful dried boletus mushrooms imported from Chile. Most supermarkets carry at least one type of dried mushroom. Since they are sometimes sandy and larger than bite-sized, dried mushrooms are usually soaked and chopped before they are cooked. Always use the flavor-packed soaking liquid for preparing the dish. If you wish, pass the liquid through a coffee filter to assure the elimination of all grit.

Mustard seeds, brown: a spice commonly used in Indian cooking, these tiny round seeds develop an appealing smoky taste when toasted. They also add attractive dots of color and crunch. Look for them in Indian markets or mail-order them from Penzeys.

Niçoise olives: small, dark, French brine-cured olives packed in olive oil.

Nuts: Since nuts have a high oil content, freeze them in a well-sealed container to avoid rancidity. Toasting nuts enhances their flavor and crispness. *To toast nuts:* Spread them out in one layer on a baking tray and set them in a toaster oven or standard oven preheated to 350°F. Toast until they turn a shade darker and/or emit a fragrant aroma, stirring every few minutes and watching carefully to avoid burning, 3 to 7 minutes depending on size and type of nut.

Orange zest: see lemon zest.

Parmesan cheese: opt for the best-quality Italian Parmigiano-Reggiano. For optimum taste, purchase a chunk and grate it as needed. Refrigerate the chunk wrapped in wax paper covered with aluminum foil. Store leftover grated cheese in a well-sealed container in the freezer.

Parsnip: a root vegetable that looks like an ancient, ivory carrot but is both sweeter and starchier. Peel or scrub parnips. (Leaving the peel intact keeps the chunks from "melting" into a puree.) If the top chunk is very thick, cut it in half for even cooking.

Pecorino Romano: a hard, aged sheep's milk cheese with a distinctive pungent flavor and considerable saltiness. It adds superb taste to rustic dishes and is less expensive than the best Parmesan. For optimum flavor, buy in a chunk and grate as needed. Refrigerate the chunk wrapped in wax paper covered with aluminum foil. Store grated leftovers in a well-sealed container in the freezer.

Pernod: a sweet licorice-flavored liqueur popular in the South of France. A few drops add marvelous flavor to fish and seafood dishes. Pernod is available in any well-stocked liquor store.

Plantains: banana look-alikes, which may be purchased and cooked at any stage of ripeness, from lime green to yellow to blackened; they become sweeter and less starchy as they ripen. To peel, slice off both ends, then make 4 or 5 incisions all along the length. Pull off the peel in strips. Plantains at any stage of ripeness cannot be eaten raw.

Polenta: The recipes call for quick-cooking polenta, which can be served as a porridge or used as a thickener for stews. Look for this cornmeal product in boxes labeled "instant" or "precooked maize meal." These products cook in 5 minutes or less. Recommended brands include Valsugana and Tipiak.

Porcini mushrooms, dried: These Italian boletus mushrooms are expensive, but have intensely delicious flavor. I've been happy with the packaged Urbani brand available in gourmet shops and the high-quality porcini I've ordered by mail from Marche aux Delices.

Portobello mushrooms (portobellas): large, full-flavored mushrooms that some consider the "steaks" of the vegetable kingdom. If you've purchased them in plastic wrap, remove the wrap as soon as you get home. If not using within a few hours, refrigerate in a basket lightly draped with a paper towel or pack them loosely in a paper bag. Use portobello mushrooms as quickly as possible. To prepare for cooking, trim off the stem's earthy root, and lightly wipe the surfaces with a damp cloth, then proceed as directed in the recipe. It is not necessary to remove the gills from the underside of the cap.

Potatoes: The recipes call primarily for Yukon Golds since they are an all-purpose variety that is readily available. If you have easy access to more flavorful potatoes, substitute them by all means. I like the flavor of potato skins, so I rarely bother to peel potatoes even though the pressure cooker doesn't tenderize the skins completely. If you prefer peeled potatoes, keep in mind that the peel on cooked potatoes slips off very easily. In recipes that call for stacking potatoes on top of the other ingredients, it makes sense to peel them after cooking.

Pumpkin seeds: Purchase these flat and tasty olive-green seeds already shelled and store them in the freezer for up to 3 months. *To toast pumpkin seeds:* Pop them into a toaster oven or a standard oven at 350°F until they puff up, about 2 minutes. Or dry-toast the seeds by stirring them in a cast-iron skillet set over medium-high heat.

Quinoa: a small, quick-cooking grain native to the Andes. Swish vigorously in several changes of water (until the water remains almost clear) to remove any residue of saponin, its natural bitter coating. Buy in health-food stores or mail-order from Gold Mine Natural Food Co.

Red bell pepper, roasted: To roast using a gas stove, place one pepper on the grid over each burner. Turn the flame to high and roast until the pepper is completely blackened and charred on the underside. Give the pepper a quarter turn with a pair of long tongs. (Avoid forks or skewers, which pierce the pepper and release the juices.) Continue to roast and turn until the pepper is charred all around. Alternatively, roast the peppers under a broiler, turning as needed. Lightly wrap the roasted peppers in wet paper towels and set aside until cool enough to handle, or longer. Rub off the blackened skin onto the paper towel. Cut the peppers in half and remove the seeds and ribs. If not using immediately, place in a sealed container, cover with a thin layer of olive oil, and refrigerate for up to 1 week.

Rice vermicelli (*bi fun, mi fun, meekrob* noodles): These angel-hair-thin rice noodles are precooked and become tender after cooking in boiling liquid for 2 to 4 minutes. (For purposes of this book, ignore any package directions about frying them.) If cooking them separately, as soon as they are done, drain and rinse them under cold water to prevent overcooking. Look for them in Asian groceries and health-food stores. It's most economical to buy them in 1-pound packages, which are usually divided into four "skeins" of noodles, making for easier handling. If you can find only the thicker rice-stick noodles, cook them according to package directions. Or substitute angel hair pasta.

Rutabaga (swede, Swedish turnip): a large yellow turnip with a purplish top. Most are heavily coated with wax to retard spoilage. Large ones can be tricky to cube. First, peel and trim. Then slice enough off one side to create a flat base. Turn the rutabaga onto this flat base and, using a sharp chef's knife, cut slices of the thickness required in the recipe. Stack the slices and cut into strips, then into cubes of the appropriate size.

Saffron threads: The stamens of crocus, these rust-colored filaments are quite costly, but a pinch goes a long way toward infusing a dish with golden color and intense flavor. Saffron can be tricky to measure: Just press the threads into a measuring spoon or guestimate by eye. To extract maximum flavor, crumble the threads and steep for a few minutes in warm water as directed in the recipe.

Sausage: see andouille, chorizo, Italian sausage, kielbasa, and linguiça.

Savoy cabbage: a green head cabbage with lacy leaves much appreciated in Italian and German kitchens. If it's not available, substitute regular green head cabbage.

Scallions: I treat scallions as two vegetables: I cook the sliced white bulb and light green stalk as I would an onion, and add the thinly sliced dark green leaves for color and mild flavor at the end of cooking. In some parts of the country, scallions are referred to as green onions.

Sesame oil, toasted: an intensely flavored oil extracted from toasted sesame seeds—a little goes a long way. Since it burns easily, toasted sesame oil is usually added at the end of cooking rather than used for an initial sauté. Available in health-food stores and Asian markets. Refrigerate once opened.

Sesame seeds: Because they are about 50 percent oil, these tiny seeds are very perishable. Freeze them in a tightly sealed container for up to 4 months. *To toast:* Scatter the seeds in a shallow baking dish and place in a toaster (or standard) oven set at 350°F until the seeds turn a shade darker, 2 to 4 minutes. You may also dry-toast them in a cast-iron skillet set over medium heat. Careful: They burn easily.

Shiitake mushrooms, dried: These intensely flavored mushrooms, sometimes called "Chinese black mushrooms," are cultivated on oak logs, then dried in the sun. The stems are quite woody and too fibrous to eat. They must be finely ground before being included in the dish; otherwise, use the whole stems for flavoring an Asian-style stock.

Swiss chard: a large, leafy green that tends to be sandy, so wash well in several changes of water. The stems have a celery-like flavor and a slightly fibrous texture, and require more cooking than the dark green leaves. You may use either green or ruby chard in the recipes.

Tahini (sesame paste): a rich paste made of ground sesame seeds. I like the Joyva brand, sold in Middle Eastern and specialty groceries. Refrigerate once opened.

Tamari: a Japanese fermented soy sauce whose quality and flavor vary according to the quality of ingredients and the aging process. I like Eden organic tamari, manufactured by traditional methods in Japan, and available in health-food stores. You may also use the Japanese soy sauce called *shoyu.* Avoid Chinese soy sauce, which is more intensely salty and has a less complex flavor.

Tomato paste: although the tubes are handy, it is more economical to purchase tomato paste in cans. Freeze leftovers in one-tablespoon heaps on a baking sheet lined with waxed paper. Once they're frozen, transfer the spoonfuls to a zipper-topped freezer bag. Add the amount you need directly to a pot of hot ingredients and the paste will dissolve quickly.

Tomatoes, diced (canned): A convenient alternative to canned whole plum tomatoes, diced tomatoes are different from the product labeled "chopped" tomatoes, which are mashed rather than diced into discrete pieces. The Eden brand, available in health-food stores, is organic and tastes closer to a freshly diced tomato than other brands I've tried. You'll also find diced tomatoes under the Muir Glen, Rotel, and other labels.

Tomatoes, diced with green chiles (canned): This canned tomato product contains diced jalapeño chiles and makes a terrific addition to Mexican and Southwestern recipes. Available under the Eden, Muir Glen, and Rotel labels; you may substitute Mexican-style tomatoes with chipotles, but do not use tomato products that contain vinegar, such as salsas.

Tomatoes, Mexican style (canned): stewed tomatoes seasoned with garlic, cumin, and oregano.

Turkey broth: a fine alternative to chicken broth when a fuller-flavored broth is appropriate. I'm not aware of any commercial product, but you can easily make your own (page 16).

Turnips: whitish, globe-shaped root vegetables with a pale purple top. Select firm, unblemished turnips. Peeling is a must since the skin on most turnips is bitter.

Veal broth: a delicate and rich broth available frozen under the Perfect Addition label (page 13) or make your own (page 19).

Vegetable broth: if you're not using homemade (page 20), try Vogue Vege Base, the broth powder sold in bulk at health-food stores under the Frontier label, or Perfect Addition frozen concentrate (page 13).

Wheat berries: the whole grain of wheat with only the outer hull removed. Wheat berries are quite chewy, even when thoroughly cooked. Look for them in health-food stores.

MAIL-ORDER SOURCES

Most of the following companies offer free catalogs on request. Many of them are extremely informative.

Adriana's Caravan
Good source for a wide variety of ethnic ingredients; also carries dried herbs, spices, and spice blends.
800-316-0820

CMC Company
Ingredients for Mexican and Asian cooking, including dried chiles and rice vermicelli.
800-CMC-2780

Corralitos Market & Sausage Company
Polish, Italian, Cajun and almost any other kind of sausage you can imagine. Also sells smoked ham and turkey.
408-722-2633

D'Artagnan
Superb gourmet sausages and free-range chickens.
800-327-8246

Gold Mine Natural Food Co.
One-stop shopping for the finest heirloom organic beans and grains (including black barley and quinoa) selected by owner Jean Richardson.
800-475-3663

Indian Harvest / Bean Bag
A wide variety of high-quality heirloom beans and grains.
800-845-2326

Marche aux Delices
Excellent dried mushrooms.
888-547-5471

Penzeys, Ltd
You'll quickly get hooked on their premium dried herbs, spices, and blends and their chatty, informative catalog.
414-679-7207

Vogue Vege Base

Good-quality instant vegetable broth powder.

888-236-4144

WoodPrairie Farm

If you're tired of Yukon Golds, join their potato-of-the month club and enjoy the many organic varieties.

800-829-9765

Zabar's

Cookware (including a variety of pressure cookers) at discount prices, including the garlic press I like and the 7-inch springform pan used for making cheesecake.

800-697-6301

Zingerman's

A fun-to-read catalog filled with the best olive oils, vinegars, and other premium gourmet ingredients selected by knowledgeable taster Ari Weinzweig.

888-636-8162

DIRECTORY OF PRESSURE-COOKER MANUFACTURERS

To obtain purchasing information and customer service, here's an alphabetical listing of manufacturers and distributors:

Aeternum
800-645-6360

Fagor
800-207-0806

Hawkins Futura
800-657-4416

Innova
319-386-6201

Kuhn-Rikon
800-662-5882

Magafesa
888-787-9991

Manttra
310-672-4227

Mirro
800-518-6245

Presto
800-877-0441

Salton
800-233-9054

Sitram
800-969-2518

T-Fal
800-395-8325

TROUBLESHOOTING

Until you get well acquainted with the pressure cooker, its behavior may occasionally puzzle you. Here are some explanations for things that may happen. **Always turn off the heat and release all pressure before attempting to remove the lid to investigate.**

■

JT = jiggle-top cooker
SG = second-generation cooker

The cooker is taking a long time to come up to pressure.

- You are cooking a larger quantity of food than usual. Be patient.

- There is insufficient liquid. Add an additional ¼ to ½ cup as needed.

- The cooker is filled well beyond the recommended capacity and there is not sufficient space for the steam pressure to gather. Cook the ingredients in two batches.

- You may need a new rubber gasket. Try lightly coating it with vegetable oil.

JT: The vent is clogged with a particle of food. Quick-release the pressure, then remove the lid and clean thoroughly.

SG: The pressure regulator is not screwed in tightly. Quick-release the pressure and check under the lid.

Water is dripping down the sides of the cooker.

- You may need a new rubber gasket. First try lightly coating it with vegetable oil.

SG: You have forgotten to lower the heat after reaching high pressure and the gasket has extruded to release excess pressure. Quick-release the pressure. Set the gasket in place and return to high pressure. Lower the heat to maintain high pressure and proceed as directed in the recipe.

Liquid or foam is spouting from the vent.

■ Immediately turn off the heat. Do not attempt to move the cooker until the pressure comes down naturally. Consider the following possibilities: You forgot to turn down the heat after reaching high pressure. Or, you did not lower the heat sufficiently and pressure kept building. If either of these is true, return to high pressure and then immediately lower the heat.

■ The cooker is too full. Cook the ingredients in two batches.

■ The food inside (probably beans or grains) is creating excess foam. After releasing the pressure, stir in a tablespoon of oil. Make certain that the vent is clean, and resume cooking.

It's difficult to get the lid to lock in place.

■ Check the locking mechanism to make sure it is functioning properly.

■ Wash and thoroughly dry the gasket. Coat it lightly with vegetable oil. If this doesn't help, replace the gasket.

It's difficult to get the lid off after the pressure has been released.

■ A vacuum has been created inside the cooker. Either wait until the cooker cools entirely or bring it back up to pressure and quick-release. The lid should come off easily.

Food either forms a crust or burns on the bottom of the cooker.

■ Use a Flame Tamer (see page 4).

■ Increase the liquid slightly the next time you cook this recipe.

■ If you've done an initial browning, be sure that no ingredients (such as onions or garlic) are sticking to the bottom.

■ Avoid stirring after adding tomatoes.

INDEX